HEALING EARTHBOUND EAGLES

HEALING EARTHBOUND EAGLES

Rodney Kingstone

WORD PUBLISHING
WORD ENTERTAINMENT LTD
Milton Keynes, England

HEALING EARTHBOUND EAGLES

First published 2000 by Word Publishing, 9 Holdom Avenue, Bletchley, Milton Keynes, Bucks, MK1 1QR, UK

1-86024-387-8

Produced for Word Publishing by Silver Fish Publishing, London.

CONTENTS

DEDICATION

To my grandchildren:
Samuel Beadle, who has given me so much happiness
and pleasure in life. You are truly a gift from God.
And Abigail Beadle, who began life with such trauma,
but is a living answer to prayer.

Also to all the leaders and members of Christian
Fellowship, Columbia, Missouri, USA.
I will always be grateful to you for the love and
friendship you have so abundantly given me.

ACKNOWLEDGEMENTS

Graham Perrins, who opened my eyes to the
glorious possibilities of the prophetic.
Peter Stott, whose loyal friendship has been
a source of continuous strength.
Dave and Rosie Fellingham, who seem to
understand me – a miracle.
Alun Davies, a man of the highest integrity who
constantly speaks encouragement to me.

FOREWORD

I first began prophesying in 1974. In the intervening years, I have seen many, many prophetic people fall by the wayside for a wide variety of reasons. Without the right environment, longevity in this ministry is extremely difficult. The prophetic ministry is hard. For every one who survives the testing, hardship, loneliness and the demonic attacks, dozens of others die out.

Comparing the prophetic ministry to other 'word' ministries is both hurtful and demoralising. Preachers and teachers can draw on a variety of elements to put across their message. Logic, reason, enthusiasm, humour, statistics and facts will provide satisfactory information to the soul, and also, under the anointing, will feed the inner man of the spirit. They will appeal to people's minds, emotions and wills. Their output is measurable and objective.

Prophets have fewer options. They must depend on revelation and the supernatural. They are often left hanging on the cross of other people's subjectivity. When logic and reason are applied to supernatural utterances, instead of the language of faith, it is hard not to feel frustrated and misunderstood.

It is too easy to silence the messenger if the word they bring is unpalatable. Do we want earthbound establishment prophets, or revelatory eagles? The role of prophetic ministry is to attack mediocrity, stimulate spiritual growth and provoke God's people to faith and sacrifice.

In the warfare that surrounds us, it is easy for churches to lose direction and purpose. In this revival season, we are all heading into uncharted territory, where there are no route maps: only a compass heading. The prophetic ministry, therefore, has become most vital as the church learns how to be led by the Spirit and not just good ideas. Reasoned approaches must give way to prophetic expression. God did not write a book then lose his voice! We need to grow people capable of supernatural speech.

Spiritual growth is encouraged by creating suitable environments. Developing the prophetic gift and ministry requires training, practice and secure family conditions. Most prophetic mistakes occur through ignorance. These mistakes are enhanced and entrenched through lack of feedback and poor discipleship.

P.I.T. is an acronym for Prophets in Training. Many people have fallen into a hole and are unable to extricate themselves without affirmation and relational support. They need a loving and generous partnership so that they can be relaxed, and released to hear the word of the Lord. I thank God for my own church, which has a large prophetic team, continuously updated training, and strong leadership acceptance and approval, with an empowering culture of discipleship.

I love Rodney because he does not hide. It takes a man of integrity to write such a book as Healing Earthbound Eagles. I really appreciate his even-handed approach. This book is an excellent tool for leaders, a good manual for prophetic ministries and churches who want to understand the pressure cooker in which prophets have to operate. It is packed with wisdom, pragmatic insights and clear experience. It is biblical, relevant and very, very timely – a must for all budding prophetic ministries and leaders, who wish to provide a support framework. It will be required reading in all my prophetic schools.

Graham Cooke, author of, *A Divine Confrontation* . . . *Birthpangs of the New Church* and *Developing Your Prophetic Gifting.*

INTRODUCTION

In the history of the Church, from the day of Pentecost to now, two prevailing conditions seem to have always preceded an outbreak of the prophetic ministry. These have been either when the Church has become utterly decadent or when there has been an outpouring of the Holy Spirit. In the latter case, prophetic ministry was not always called by this name, but investigation shows that during such outpourings, revelation was both received by people and given by them. It should not surprise us that, at times of an outpouring of the Spirit, there is also an increase in prophetic ministry.

The ability of God's people to prophesy is the mark of the age of the Spirit in which we are all living. Peter makes this very clear in his explanation of the day of Pentecost in Acts chapter 2. In verses sixteen to eighteen Peter, quoting from Joel 2:28–29, inserts the extra line 'and they will prophesy'. Why is this? Is he deliberately misquoting Joel? Has he had a memory lapse? The answer is: neither of these. It is his way of calling attention to something important. He cannot underline the words in red ink or speak them in upper case lettering, but he can repeat the same phrase at the end of a section as he has used at the beginning ie 'will prophesy'. The way the Bible points out the importance

13

of a passage is to begin and end the passage with the same phrase. When Peter is speaking it is his way of saying 'pay attention to this, it is important'. The important point that Peter is emphasising is this: now the Holy Spirit has come, all of the redeemed community baptised in him can prophesy. This had never been possible before. In times past, the Holy Spirit came upon prophets and kings and other significant individuals and they prophesied: but never before had it been possible for all of God's people to do so.

The day of Pentecost changed all that and brought into being the desire that Moses had for the people of God. This desire is expressed in Numbers 11:29: 'But Moses replied, "Are you jealous for my sake? I wish that all the Lord's people were prophets and that the Lord would put his Spirit on them!"' The context of the verse is this: Moses had appointed seventy elders to assist him in leading the people of Israel. He then took them to the tent of meeting, that place where God would come and speak with Moses face to face, and the Lord took of the Spirit that was upon Moses and put the Spirit upon the elders, who immediately prophesied (but never prophesied again as far as we are told). However, two of the elders Eldad and Medad did not go to the tent of meeting, but remained in the camp and prophesied. Upon hearing this, Joshua, who was with Moses, said, 'Moses, my lord, stop them!' Moses replied, 'I wish that all the Lord's people were prophets [would prophesy] and that the Lord would put his Spirit upon them!' This statement was more than Moses' personal desire: he was expressing God's heart and desire. Moses was a prophet. He calls himself one: 'The Lord your God will raise up for you a prophet like me' (Deut. 18:15). Scripture also says he was one: 'The Lord used a prophet to bring Israel up from Egypt, by a prophet he cared for him' (Hos. 12:13).

In his capacity as a prophet, Moses is, therefore, revealing God's desire in having all his people prophesy: a desire that could never be fulfilled under the old covenant, but became a glorious possibility under the new covenant. This possibility was publicly proclaimed on the day of Pentecost when the Holy Spirit was poured out upon all flesh.

Now all the Lord's people can prophesy, whether old or young, male or female. The apostle Paul makes the same assertion in 1 Corinthians 14. In verse 1 of this chapter, he tells his readers to eagerly desire the gift of prophecy. This must be because the gift is available to them, otherwise he is creating a false expectation, together with frustration, by exhorting all of them to eagerly desire (strive after zealously), to prophesy knowing that some, or most, will not be able to. In verse 5, he wants everyone to prophesy and, in verse 24, envisages a meeting where everyone is prophesying. If God did not intend everyone to prophesy, then the section contained in verses 22–25 is meaningless, as such a scenario could not possibly take place. In verse 31, he says, 'you can all prophesy in turn'. The restriction contained in verse 29 about two or three prophets speaking is not a limit upon the number of prophecies in a meeting, but a pragmatic pause after every two or three prophetic words in order that, where appropriate, they can be weighed by the others present. Finally, in verse 39, concluding this teaching, he again tells his readers to be eager to prophesy. The importance of this passage in showing that all may prophesy, and the correct usage of prophecy and tongues, is emphasised by Paul beginning and ending the chapter with the same phrase, 'be eager to prophesy'.

However, whilst all believers baptised in the Holy Spirit can prophesy, it does not mean that all Spirit-baptised believers will have a prophetic ministry, or be prophets. Prophetic ministry differs from simply exercising the gift of prophecy in this way: the gift of prophecy, as we have seen, is open to all believers, but will, in practice, probably be exercised infrequently by any one person. In contrast, the person with a prophetic ministry will usually exercise a frequent use of the gift of prophecy and have an understanding of God's corporate purposes. They will often experience dreams/visions and move in other gifts like words of knowledge and words of wisdom, which enhance their prophetic gifting. It is to these people in particular, that this book is addressed, although others will find principles contained in it that will definitely be of benefit to them.

Chapter 1

PROPHETIC PEOPLE ARE EAGLES

It should be no surprise at all that when the church has been utterly decadent, there has been an increase in prophetic ministry. It was the increasing worldliness in the church, together with the replacing of spiritual power by learning amongst the leaders, that gave rise to the Montanist's in AD 156. These people saw a renewal of the gift of prophecy. Although some of their prophetic utterances left much to be desired, they taught and practised much needed reform, numbering amongst them such champions as Irenaeus and Tertullian. In both conditions referred to – either the church being decadent or an outpouring of the Spirit – God revealed something of his heart, mind, will and purpose for the church, together with a revelation of her destiny and identity. This has been true for the universal as well as for the local church. The reason for this outbreak of prophetic ministry in the situations described, is in order to bring a decadent church back to true life and to restore it to the glorious church that God desires. In the case of an outpouring of the Spirit, the prophetic breaks out in order to keep the church on course and to establish within it the purposes of God. In both situations, the outbreak of prophetic ministry is not simply to be an initial experience that, having accomplished the above purposes, can then diminish. It is to be a regular part of the life of the church: constantly bringing to that church strength, encouragement and comfort (1 Cor. 14:3).

It should, therefore, come as no surprise to us that Satan would seek to hinder the expression of the prophetic in and to the church. Obviously, he prefers a decadent church to one that is moving in the will and purposes of God, so he will oppose the prophetic in order to keep the church in its sorry state. He also seeks to hinder the church from realising the will and purposes of God in times of outpouring, by opposing the prophetic. Prophetic people, therefore, become a prime target for him. A. W. Tozer once said that Satan desires unlimited power over the human family and whenever he is challenged by the Spirit of God he invariably retaliates with savage fury. Prophetic ministry will always challenge evil ambition wherever it is found, just as it will challenge any attempt at dominion other than the rightful dominion of God and his kingdom in the earth.

Whatever means Satan uses to assault prophetic people, the purpose of such an assault remains the same. That is, to stop them receiving revelation and then to stop them proclaiming it. The result of this in their lives will be akin to keeping an eagle earthbound. There will be frustration and restriction, instead of fulfilment and freedom. Fulfilment in being who they are and performing their God-given task. Freedom in being able to soar to the heights in the presence of God and freedom in delivering his prophetic word in the presence of people. Prophetic people are God's spiritual 'eagles'.

This can be clearly illustrated by looking at the parallels that exist between the references to eagles in Scripture and prophetic people. Deuteronomy chapter 32 records the song of Moses, in which Moses, amongst other things, speaks of God's leading and care for the Children of Israel in the wilderness. Verses 11–12 state: 'like an eagle that stirs up its nest and hovers over its young, that spreads its wings to catch them and carries them on its pinions. The Lord alone led him; no foreign god was with him.' However, in Hosea 12:13, where the prophet is speaking of the Exodus and the subsequent wilderness experience, he says, 'The Lord used a prophet to bring Israel up from Egypt, by a prophet he cared for him'. Clearly it was God's initiative and God who was leading, but this was expressed through Moses who is called a prophet here and in Deuteronomy 18:18.

Returning then to Deuteronomy 32:11, the eagle likeness must primarily refer to God, but in a secondary capacity it can also refer to Moses (the prophet) and the way, under God's direction, that he led and cared for Israel. God led Israel through Moses, and Moses led Israel through God's direction. The eagle is pictured as stirring up the nest, hovering over its young and catching and carrying them on its wings. This is what happens when it is time for the young eaglets to fly. The parent eagle stirs up the nest to excite the young ones to fly, thrusting the young into the air, she hovers over them and as they flounder, she swoops underneath them and bears them up on her wings. The parent eagle is saying that it is time to grow up and move on, but at the same time initially keeping a caring eye upon them. In a word, the eagle is motivating them. This is one aspect of the prophetic ministry. To stir or motivate people to action. It is given in order that the church may not lose momentum and become static.

The church is meant to be on the move, advancing the Kingdom of God, not static, maintaining the status quo. Jesus himself spoke of this in the 'great commission': 'All authority in heaven and on earth has been given to me. Therefore go and make disciples of all nations, baptising them in the name of the Father and of the Son and of the Holy Spirit, and teaching them to obey everything I have commanded you' (Matt. 28:18–20). The whole thrust of the text is one of dynamic advancement. We are supposed to be moving on, fulfilling the purposes of God, not settling down.

The prophetic stirs up that which has settled down. The book of Haggai provides us with a vivid example of this. The remnant that had returned to Jerusalem from the captivity in Babylon had begun well on their work of rebuilding the temple. Then, for various reasons, the work on the temple ceased and the people became more concerned with building their own houses. About fifteen years further on, Haggai the prophet, together with Zechariah, came and began prophesying to the people about this. The result was that the Lord stirred up the spirit of the people and they recommenced the work of rebuilding the temple (Ezra 5:1–2; Hag. 1:14). The Hebrew word for stir used in Haggai, is the same word that is used in Deuteronomy 32:11 of the eagle stirring up the nest. Prophetic people are needed in order to stop the church from settling down and accepting the status quo instead of rising up and moving into all God has for it.

These stirrings by prophetic people are not always comfortable to live with. They challenge us and most of us do not like to be challenged. We prefer to be left alone to get on with life as usual. We like to remain in the safe confines of our comfort zones, rather than be stretched by moving into areas of uncharted spiritual experience. Like the people to whom Haggai prophesied, we want to live comfortably in our cosy houses, but God's agenda is different. He wants his house built as the priority. If that house, then, is to be built correctly, prophetic ministry must be released. Ephesians 2:20 reminds us that the church is built upon the foundation of the Apostles and Prophets. In chapter 4 verse 12, the ministry of the prophet is given (along with the other mentioned ministries) 'to prepare God's people for works of service, so that the body of Christ may be built up . . . and become mature'. Just like the eagle, in Deuteronomy 32, that in essence says 'it is time to grow up' so prophetic ministry should play a vital role in bringing the church into maturity.

When the prophetic is held in abeyance, then a powerful means of motivating the people of God is lost. This also holds true in the realm of prayer. Unfortunately, it is all too easy for prayer to fall into a predictable and sometimes boring routine. This is a tragedy, for the very nature of prayer is that it should be anything but boring and predictable. It should be dynamic, because one is addressing the living God. How different it is when the prophetic word brings direction and revelation to our prayers. That which was routine, becomes an adventure with the Spirit of God, as hearts are stirred to pray in alignment with God's will. At the conclusion of Paul's teaching on spiritual warfare and the armour of God, (Eph. 6:10–18), he speaks of praying with all kinds of prayers. He is saying that when engaged in spiritual warfare, we need to know what kind of prayers to use in any given situation. The prophetic ministry 'stirs' us to pray and brings revelation of what kind of praying we are to do.

When the Lord spoke to Jeremiah (Jer. 7:16), and told him not to pray for the people of Judah because of their idolatry, he mentions in that verse four different kinds of prayer: 'pray', 'plea', 'petition', and 'plead'. For each of these words, the Hebrew has a distinct meaning. They are not different terms for the same thing; they are different kinds of prayer.

The word *pray* means to act as a mediator between judge and criminal. This is prayer where we ask God to have mercy upon those who deserve his judgement. Both Abraham and Moses engaged in this kind of prayer when God told them he would bring judgement upon Sodom and Gomorrah in the case of Abraham, and that he would destroy the children of Israel in the case of Moses. When God revealed this to his two servants, both of them immediately began to ask for mercy to be granted to the offending parties. Again, when Amos receives from the Lord two visions of impending judgement upon the people, he immediately asks the Lord to forgive them and to stop these kinds of judgement (Amos 7:1–6). These men of God intervened in prayer between God and the objects of his just punishment.

The word *plea*, however, means a shout of joy or grief. The shout of joy is prayer by praise. David says, in Psalm 138:1, 'I will praise you O Lord, with all my heart; before the 'gods' I will sing your praise'. Here is no mystical binding of 'demonic gods' here is the shout of praise for the wonderful works of God and his greatness that breaks strongholds and restrains evil ones (Ps. 149). On the other hand, the shout of grief is the entering into the heart of God and experiencing something of his feelings towards the hurting, broken and outcasts of the world. It is akin to the inarticulate groans of the Spirit, in Romans 8:26. Dr. Ed Miller told me of an occasion, during the Argentinean revival in the 1940's, when a lady of his church knocked on his door and upon opening it he found her sobbing and distraught. Inviting her in, it took some time before she could compose herself enough to speak, being in such great distress. He assumed that some awful tragedy must have struck her or her family, but when she eventually spoke she said, 'Pastor, I have just seen a drunk man'. Dr. Miller told me he was so cross inside and wanted to tell the lady not to be so stupid and to pull herself together. At that instant, the Holy Spirit said to him, 'She saw the drunk with my eyes'. The cry of grief is a powerful prayer on behalf of those who have no help and do not know where to turn.

The word *petition* means strong, incessant pleadings. Not giving up until one receives the answer. This is not a case of trying to twist God's arm by keeping on at him, but we keep on at him because he listens to us. The parable Jesus taught, in Luke 18:1–8, of the persistent widow who kept on asking an unjust judge for justice against her adversary, is not a picture of God's reluctance being overcome by our persistence. It is a parable of contrast. God is not reluctant, he is ever mindful and listening to the cries of his own – to which, in time, he will respond – but he wants us to always pray and not give up. We do not keep praying in order to get him to listen, but because he listens, we keep on praying.

It is the tenacity of a Jacob who cries, 'I will not let you go unless you bless me' (Gen. 32:26). David Wang of Asian Outreach based in Hong Kong, told me of the time he was called to pray for a dying girl in a hospital in the Philippines. When he arrived at the hospital, he found the lifeless little girl being cradled in her mother's arms in a side room. She had died before he got there. He then told her parents that they were going to pray, and for the next few hours, he and the parents cried out to God for the life of the child. He then believed that God had heard them and that they were no longer to ask, but to thank God for her life. Leaving the hospital, because he had a conference meeting to address that night, he reiterated to the parents that they should keep thanking God for the answer. He was in the middle of preaching his message that night, when the door of the hall opened and in walked the parents carrying the little girl, who was now very much alive. I can still feel the tremendous impact of the Spirit when he leaned towards me and said, 'You see Rodney, many Christians give up too soon'. You stop when God tells you to stop because the answer is no, or you stop when you know he has given you the assurance that the matter is done: never do you stop only upon an assumption.

Finally, the word *plead* means to intercede, to entreat. It is identifying with the people or person for whom one is praying. The highest example of this is the Lord Jesus himself, who ever lives to make intercession for us (Heb. 7:25), the very ones with whom he identified when he took not the form of angels, but came in the likeness of men (Heb. 2:16). The great intercessory prayers of the Old Testament are to be found in Ezra 9, Nehemiah 9, and Daniel 9. In each record, the common element is the identifying, by prayer, with the condition of the people being prayed for.

Now how are we to know which form of prayer we should use, in order to be the most effective in any given situation? God's answer is to make it known to us by revelation through the prophetic gift. He stirs us to pray and shows us how to pray through his prophetic eagles.

There is another aspect of prophetic ministry that is likened to the eagle, in Deuteronomy 32:11, and that is caring. The eagle hovers over its young and spreads its wings to catch them. Unfortunately, prophetic people have often been caricatured as the very opposite of caring sensitive people. They have been perceived as bold, insensitive and uncaring; only interested in delivering the word. Nothing should be further from the truth. In 1 Corinthians 14:3, Paul speaks of the three results that a prophetic word should bring about in people lives: they should be strengthened, encouraged and comforted. This sounds far more like caring than anything else. Jesus wonderfully demonstrated this caring aspect of prophetic ministry when he delivered his prophetic word of judgement over Jerusalem with such pathos and tears in his eyes (Luke 19:41–44). Here there was no hint of pleasure at their coming 'just deserts', but a heart full of caring compassion. This is not to be confused with sentimentality. No Pharisee or Sadducee on the end of one of Jesus' rebukes would ever have thought him sentimental. The reason Jesus spoke so vehemently to them was that he cared about the people who were being so adversely affected by their teachings and practice: not to mention the care he had, to see that Scripture was rightly adhered to and that his father was correctly portrayed. Care was an important part of the ministry of Jesus the prophet par excellence. So when the time came for the prophetic judgement to be proclaimed over Jerusalem the word was strong but the attitude in delivery was one of care.

This aspect of caring in the prophetic ministry is also seen in the life and ministry of Moses. As mentioned before, Hosea says of Moses: 'The Lord used a prophet to bring Israel up from Egypt, by a prophet he cared for him' (Hos. 12:13). The Hebrew word for cared (shamar) means to keep, guard, protect, save life, watch, wait, take heed or beware. All of these meanings were exercised in the ministry of Moses towards Israel.

Principally, he carried them out through prophetic words given to the people who came to him (Exod. 18:13–27). These prophetic words would be either an application to the case before him of God's statutes and laws or a word of revelation received direct from the Lord that would give an answer to the person's query or situation. The result was that the people were fed, guided and protected. They were undoubtedly aware of being cared for. Prophetic people also care for the body of Christ and the individuals that make up that body. That is why Paul says, 'he who prophesies edifies (builds up) the church' (1 Cor. 14:4) and 'you can all prophesy in turn so that everyone may be instructed and encouraged' (v.31). You cannot reflect the caring heart of God to his people while, at the same time, being uncaring or diffident yourself.

The book of Job also makes reference to eagles in chapter 39 verses 27–29: 'Does the eagle soar at your command and build his nest on high? He dwells on a cliff and stays there at night; a rocky crag is his stronghold. From there he seeks out his food; his eyes detect it from afar.' The first thing the verse states is that eagles are not controlled by humans. They do not soar at a man's command. This is absolutely fundamental in prophetic ministry, for, as Peter records in 2 Peter 1:21, 'prophecy never had its origin in the will of man, but men spoke from God as they were carried along by the Holy Spirit.' Prophetic people do not originate their words. Their words (their revelatory meaning) are given them by the Holy Spirit who then bears them along. That is, they continue speaking as long as he is inspiring, but when he finishes, they finish. Furthermore, they do not respond to human commands to give prophetic words, nor do they respond to human desires to have a prophetic word spoken. Two phenomenal abilities of the eagle are mentioned here: the ability to soar to great heights and the ability to see clearly from afar. These two abilities are also characteristic of prophetic people. They love to soar upon the thermal of the Holy Spirit: to be lifted up, as it were, into the presence of God in worship and to momentarily leave the demands of earth in order to concentrate upon the agenda of heaven.

One of the features of prophetic people is their ability to see things from the perspective of the throne of God. They are not tied to purely human assessments of situations, they have heaven's perspective as it is revealed to them. They are at home in the heavenly realm, even as they live their life upon earth. They are certainly not so heavenly-minded as to be of no earthly use: rather they are very useful on earth because of their heavenly-mindedness. Prophetic people, therefore, know what it is like to be borne along by the Spirit and to be visionaries by the Spirit.

The church needs the prophetic to lift it in worship to new levels of appreciation of the greatness and awesomeness of God: to bring to the church the sense of God's imminence in times of worship. That is why David appointed prophets as the chief musicians for the temple. Asaph was appointed as chief of music (1 Chron. 16:5) and he was a prophet (2 Chron. 29:30). Asaph's sons, in 1 Chronicles 25:1–7, were appointed to prophesy with music. These 'musical prophets' had a twofold task. They were to build a platform by their anointed playing for the release of the prophetic and also to prophesy by their playing or accompanied by their playing. The phrase in 1 Chronicles 25:1, 'accompanied by', can mean both. However good our worship is, we must never settle at that point. We must be grateful for it and we must certainly not become intense about trying to improve it, but we must look for the moving of the prophetic to take us higher in it. By this I do not mean a constant interruption of a worship time by the gift of prophecy calling attention to our needs etc. I mean that revelation of God, communicated through the gift of prophecy, that causes us to worship him with passionate outpouring of love and allegiance.

In Revelation 19:10, when the Apostle John is about to fall down and worship an angel, the angel stops him, saying: 'Worship God! For the testimony of Jesus is the spirit of prophecy.' The Amplified Bible understands the words 'the spirit of prophecy' to mean the essence of prophecy. The essence of prophecy then, is to bear witness to Jesus. The phrase 'the spirit of prophecy' (to pneuma tes propheteias) was a common rabbinic description of the Holy Spirit. In other words, the Holy Spirit is the author of all true prophecy, which will always bear witness to Jesus. The context suggests that the spirit of prophecy will direct us to worship Jesus.

In this soaring ability in worship, that prophetic people have and seek to bring to others, the teaching element is often overlooked. Worship and prophecy are seen, at times, as the preliminaries to the preaching of the word: this preaching of the word being seen as the only really valid expression of teaching in the church. For Israel though, praise and prophecy were an acknowledged means of bringing teaching and instruction. When Moses introduced his song, in Deuteronomy 32:1–43, he said (sang), 'Listen, O heavens, and I will speak; hear, O earth, the words of my mouth. Let my teaching fall like rain and my words descend like dew'. The *teaching* contained in this song is directly quoted in more than eight passages in the New Testament.

Asaph, the prophet, composed Psalm 78 and he begins the song with, 'O my people hear my teaching'. The

Psalms are a rich deposit of teaching, from which the apostles frequently drew. No wonder, then, that Paul exhorts us in Colossians 3:16 to teach and admonish one another in psalms, hymns and spiritual songs. There should be good content in them. In studying the ways in which prophecy has been communicated to us in the Scripture, we see that songs have been regularly used and even poetry, as more than half of prophecy in the Bible is in the form of poetry, rather than just narrative. This teaching should further our appreciation of him and so draw even more worship out of our hearts. Who can sit with a small view of God and remain unmoved by such teaching as contained in Wesley's great hymn, 'And can it be that I should gain an interest in the Saviour's blood'. Similarly, prophecy that stirs us to worship should, for example, contain teaching of like manner.

Returning to our passage in Job, we also note that not only do eagles soar, but they also have amazing eyesight. They can discern their prey at great distances, or under difficult conditions. They have the ability to see the bigger picture as well as the detail. The gifting of prophetic people makes them able to see, which is one reason why the Old Testament referred to the early prophets as 'seers' (1 Sam. 9:9). They can see the panorama of God's dealings, as well as homing in upon the detail. The church needs the prophetic to paint the wider or bigger picture of God's dealings and purposes, as well as to pinpoint the detail of what needs to changed or to be incorporated. At other times, prophetic people have foresight as to the future and what our response should be. We often need to see where we fit in the wider scene of God's moving. Many are the times when we sense something is happening or about to happen, in the purposes of God and yet we do not know what we should be doing about it. Then there are those times when things are just not going right in church life and we cannot understand why or work out what is wrong. These are the times for which God has provided an answer and that answer lies in the ministry of prophetic people. (For indicators that a person is prophetic, see Chapter 9). For like the natural eagle, which can see clearly under difficult conditions, prophetic people can also 'see' under difficult conditions, because they are dependent upon revelation.

The natural circumstances cannot cloud divine revelation, no matter how hard people may try. On one occasion, I was involved with a church, when suddenly everything started going wrong: people were leaving for no good reason, the income was rapidly decreasing and the times of worship became depressing. It seemed as if a black cloud hovered over the church and nothing could remove it. Then a prophetic word came saying that there was an 'Absalom spirit' in the church and God would deal with it. Within weeks, a situation became known, which exposed a leader who had been involved in creating discord amongst the members on a wide scale. When that leader found out that he had been exposed, he hurriedly resigned and left that church before the other leaders could take any action. At the next meeting, the cloud had lifted and the worship soared again. Although the church was, by now, somewhat depleted in numbers, miraculous financial provision came their way and in a short time, people began to be added to the church. As previously said, is it any wonder, then, that Satan opposes prophetic people; attempting by many means to curtail the release of the prophetic through them.

In my travels in the ministry from the Far East through India, Europe and on to America, I have found many of God's earthbound eagles: those who no longer bring a prophetic word and those who have lost all confidence that they will ever receive a prophetic word again. I have also been in many churches that hardly ever have a prophetic word and certainly have no sense of prophetic direction. There are other churches that have prophetic words, but take little notice of them. All of these things either result in restricting God's eagles, or are the result of his prophetic eagles being earthbound.

In one church, when I was teaching a small group of prophetic people, two of the company began to weep. Upon further investigation, I discovered that both of these people had, at one time, been used in the prophetic quite frequently, but had been hurt and abused by a leader because of their gifting. So for sixteen years, they had not moved publicly in it. Truly they were now earthbound and needed to be released to soar and to see again. This release, I am happy to say, occurred before the end of the series I was taking. However, we must not see the Devil as the only reason why prophetic people become earthbound. Sometimes, prophetic people bind themselves, by failing to understand the characteristics of their temperament and also their calling. This means that they fall prey to misunderstanding and the misinterpreting of their needs, feelings, and thinking. I will say more about this in Chapter 3.

In order, then, for release to come, we must understand the reason or reasons why we have become earthbound. Make no mistake, when you are not moving in your gifting the church stops moving in its fullness. Ultimately, this is what we are after: not simply release in our ability to minister, but that through our ministering the church is blessed, strengthened, encouraged, and motivated.

Chapter 2

EARTHBOUND EAGLES AFFECT THE CHURCH

God wants his church to be blessed, strengthened, encouraged, and motivated. When the prophetic gift stays silent, then these, as well as other things, will suffer tremendously. We must, therefore, look at what the prophetic is designed to give to the local church.

Foundation Laying

Ephesians 2:20 speaks of the church being built upon the foundation of the apostles and prophets. Whilst I believe 'the prophets' in this verse refers to those functional offices of both the Old and New Testament prophet, nevertheless there is an application that applies to all prophetic ministry in the church.

Foundation laying relates to knowing who we are and where we are going. Indeed, the church can be described as a prophetic community: a people who know their identity and know their destiny. The Lord Jesus himself at an early age was both aware of his identity and his destiny (Luke 2:49) and so he laid a foundation for the prophetic community, the church, which would come into being because of and through him. That being the case, the church would, then, as a prophetic community, both express the full life of Jesus and the Kingdom of God: that is, the church would express the King and the Kingdom. To do this a foundation of truth must be laid.

This foundation of truth is essential for and at the beginning of a local church, but there are times when the church needs to be reminded or recalled to such an understanding. Unfortunately, it is too easy for a local church to forget its identity as well as it destiny. This can be its ultimate identity and destiny, or its immediate identity and destiny. Here is where the prophetic gift is needed in order to keep the church on course. One may well ask the question, 'Shouldn't the pastor/teacher be doing this?' Of course, the short, simplistic answer may seem to be 'yes' – but that is not the case. Church life is not always as simple or clear as we would like it to be. The prophetic operates by revelation, not simply when things are naturally obvious. Therefore, a church and/or its leadership may not be aware that it is losing its identity or beginning to lose its way. The prophetic messages of Jesus to the churches in the book of Revelation show this to be so. They were not without their teachers, but even so, they needed to be corrected and brought back onto the right course. So, for example, a church may start to engage itself in all kinds of commendable activities and yet not realise that these activities are not on God's agenda for that church at that present time, or even for the future. The prophetic ministry, as it reveals something of the heart, mind, will and purpose of God, brings clarity and calls the church back to its foundational calling.

Similarly, it is possible for a church to lose sight of its identity, as well as individual believers losing theirs. Who we are in Christ, what we are as a church, are truths that the prophetic needs to keep before us in order that we do not slide into false identities. Closely allied to this is the function of pulling down that which is wrong or unnecessary in the church. This was Jeremiah's prophetic mandate along, with the more positive side of building up (Jer. 1:10). Many a local church is in need of having its metaphorical building site cleared. Also, unbiblical motivation such as guilt or pride needs to be cleared away. All this is necessary if a building fit for the habitation of God is to be built. The local church needs to be uncluttered and single-minded in its vision and outworking of the purposes of God. The prophetic gift operating in the church is God's method of bringing this to pass, not the church trying to get vision and direction out of a plethora of personal but well-meaning opinions.

Vision

Prophets impart vision to the people of God. The name 'seer', as applied to early biblical prophets (1 Sam. 9:9), implies that they see things and cause others to see by their telling of what they see. My working definition of prophecy is: 'The unveiling of the heart, mind and purpose of God for or in a specific situation, or for the envisioning of a group of people or a person.' Imparting vision is an important part of the prophetic ministry to the body of Christ. Usually, when people think of vision they are thinking of that which inspires, uplifts and often liberates. They think in terms of expanding knowledge and understanding, as well as exciting motivation. All of this is true and necessary. Vision means the church keeps moving towards its God-given goals. Vision gives the people of God cohesiveness as they work towards what God has revealed to them. Vision gives the local church a purpose for existence. There is, however, another aspect of vision that people are often unaware of, but which is just as important: restraint.

Probably the most well-known verse relating to vision is Proverbs 29:18, as translated by the Authorised Version: 'Where there is no vision, the people perish'. It is worthwhile considering some other translations of this verse. The New International Version says, 'Where there is no revelation, the people cast off restraint'; the Revised Standard Version says, 'Where there is no prophecy the people cast off restraint'; the American Standard Version says, 'Where there is no vision, the people cast off restraint'; and The Jerusalem Bible says, 'Where there is no vision the people get out of hand.' Revelation, prophecy, and vision are all used here in the same way and are vital to bring the people of God into the restriction of discipline needed in order to stay within God-given boundaries. Horses need reins to prevent them from wandering wherever they wish to go and to keep to the path the rider purposes. Vision, therefore, becomes a means of keeping the people of God from wandering off after every good thought, idea, or self-imposed agenda and to stay within the guidelines of God's purposes. In the days when the Judges governed Israel, the people were an unhealthy, non-cohesive population. 'In those days Israel had no king; everyone did as he saw fit' (Judg. 21:25). This was, in part, due to the fact that 'in those days the word of the Lord was rare; there were not many visions'. What happened to a nation back then, happens to a local church in these days when the prophetic voice is rare or non-existent.

One of the great problems of the church in the West, is that of individualism. We have so emphasised the individual and personal aspect of our relationship with God, that we balk at anything which even suggests a curtailing of this for the common good. This is exactly why we need vision that is imparted through prophetic ministry. It will enable us to have the necessary restraint to keep from doing what is right in our eyes and to do that which is right in God's eyes for us as a community of redeemed people. After all, the purpose of the outpouring of the Holy Spirit on the day of Pentecost was not simply to give individuals the power to *do witnessing,* but to bring into being a corporate people who would *be a witness* to Jesus. This corporate people would have as its mark the ability to prophesy, which would, amongst other things, provide them with the vision required for both restraint and constraint in the purposes of God.

Explaining

On occasions, the prophetic will tell why things are as they are, without always telling what must change or what will be the result of any change. An example of this is found in Judges 6:7–10. Israel has been oppressed by the power of the Midianites for seven years. These Midianites have plundered and ravaged the land. The Israelites are so impoverished that they cry out to the Lord for help. What happens next is that God sends them a prophet. The prophet's message tells them why all this has happened, but does not say anything further. Of course, the implication is there that, because they have not listened to the Lord (v.10), they need to repent, but the prophet does not specifically state this. It is as if the prophet is answering Gideon's question of verse 13, 'if the Lord is with us, why has all this happened to us?' ahead of Gideon's asking. In the interview with the angel of the

Lord, Gideon receives no answer to his question. It is quite possible for God to answer our questions before we ask them. The prophetic ministry will sometimes speak ahead of the context that is required to make absolute sense of the message. That is why we must give careful attention to all prophetic utterances.

Perhaps, in situations like this in the local church, part of the responsibility of the teacher is to tell people what to do once the prophetic has revealed why things are as they are. In this way the ministries are seen to complement one another, without any one ministry being sufficient of itself for all occasions and situations. We must be careful, however, not to make boundaries around the ministry functions too definitive. Some teachers will certainly have a prophetic element at times in their teaching and those operating in the gift of prophecy will also have an instructional element in their prophesying (1 Cor. 14:31).

It is also interesting to note that, at times, in explaining the why of a situation, the prophetic person will use a passage of Scripture, or texts, to do more than simply interpret the texts. They will seek, in the texts, to interpret God's heart and the needs of people. This does not mean that the prophetic person will interpret God's word from events, but rather that they will bring understanding of the events in the light of God's word. Graham Perrins, in his *Prophetic Bulletin* No.12 July/August 1991, puts it this way:

> There is an illustration in Haggai where priests and prophet comment on the same texts and so highlight the difference in their approaches. Haggai asked the priests (who undertook teaching) for a ruling on the law relating to clean and unclean. The priest interpreted the texts

correctly, but Haggai re-interpreted them and turned them into a prophetic word for his day. Israel had complained that nothing had gone right, harvests yielded little, clothing didn't keep them warm, and wages went into purses with holes. Haggai asserts the reason was because they were unclean, and everything they touched became unclean. God's house lay desolate whilst they lived in panelled houses. Without a dwelling place, how could there be a manifestation of God's presence to sanctify Israel and set them apart as his people? Unless God's house became their priority, dissatisfaction, frustration and uncleanness would remain their lot. Haggai urged them to start work on God's house. In the light of the successful rebuilding programme established by Zerubbabel and Joshua, Israel's fortunes began to change. From the twenty-fourth day of the ninth month, three months after building had commenced, Haggai promised that God would now bless them (Hag. 1:13–15).

Here is creative, relevant exegesis of the law that goes beyond a priestly ruling. Law becomes a living word revealing God's purpose for Haggai's day. His ministry imparts not only understanding but also vision and motivation. The difference between the prophet and other ministries is not that they teach and he doesn't, but that his teaching can take many different forms and expressions.

Leon Wood, in his book *The Prophets of Israel,* differentiates between preaching and teaching. The prophet's manner of speaking, he suggests, is preaching, which has as its goal a stirring to reaction and response. It addresses the emotion and the will, whereas the teacher addresses, primarily, the mind, with the goal being to impart information. On other occasions, the prophetic will give an explanation and then go on to say what must be done or what may be expected. Ezekiel does this in chapters 14 and 18. In both, he brings an explanation to those enquiring of him and then commands them to repent if they want to see change.

The prophetic bringing explanations to a church that has lost vision, impetus, faith or is struggling to know how to handle the difficulties it is facing, will help that church enormously to focus upon the real reasons for its present state of affairs. For example, are the problems from satanic attack? If so then the church needs to stand firm and resist him and not become unhealthily introspective, looking for other causes within individual lives or the corporate body. Alternatively, if the reason is, because our lives need putting in order, then to be resisting the Devil, rebuking demons, or to be praying against the evil days in which we live, is just a waste of time. The explanation of the prophetic will direct our spiritual energy into the right path to ensure that things or people change and thus, the blessing of God can continue upon the church. This is not to say that every 'why' question we have can or will be answered by the prophetic, or any other means. Clearly there are mysteries in God and life that remain so for believers and unbelievers alike, but the truth remains that there are many circumstances in life that God wants to explain and prophetic ministry in the church is one of his chosen ways of doing this.

Another sphere of explanation that prophetic ministry brings to the church is that of showing God's prophetic purpose throughout history. The book of Revelation charts the purpose of God through history, culminating in the glorious victory of Christ and his church. This, John says, was and is clearly revealed to God's servants the prophets (Rev. 10:7). Security, assurance and faith are brought into being when people are shown the unerring hand of God moving, with purpose, in all circumstances and situations, to bring to pass his perfect plan. It is not only the universal prophetic purpose that needs to be explained, but also the local church's history. A local church is in existence because of the will of God and has a prophetic purpose for its being. Without explanation of God's purpose in its history, the local church will simply see itself as surviving and experiencing an unconnected series of events: a potpourri instead of sovereign purpose.

Predicting

The prophetic will also predict or have a predictive element at times. This is clearly seen in the New Testament in the ministry of Agabus. He foretold a coming famine and also what would befall Paul when he went to Jerusalem (Acts 11:28; 21:10). The predictive or foretelling characteristic of prophecy is not given to simply satisfy the curious as to what will happen. Neither is it given in order that we may live by sight because we know the future, thus removing the need to trust in our loving heavenly father's sovereignty. It is never to be confused with occultism's predictive goals of having power over people, or to simply reveal the unknown.

Prophecy is given in order that we may respond in some way that will result in the strengthening, encouraging or comforting of others. This is exactly what happened when Agabus prophesied the famine. The church at Antioch immediately gave money that Saul and Barnabas were to take to the elders at Jerusalem to help alleviate the poverty that would be caused by the famine. It is also given to encourage and confirm an individual's walk with God. When Agabus prophesied of

Paul's treatment and imprisonment when he went to Jerusalem, this confirmed to Paul in a very specific way what the Spirit had already been preparing him for in other cities (Acts 20:22–23). Thus, the word brought by Agabus confirmed to Paul that what he had been hearing was right and also became the means by which Paul could prepare himself for the ordeal that lay ahead. One can only speculate what would have happened in these two incidents if the prophetic word had been silent in the early church. Would the poor saints in Jerusalem have had a long wait for relief to come, communication not being what it is today? Indeed, would Antioch have even been moved to give? Would Paul have been able to fortify himself in God for the Jerusalem troubles without the prophetic word being delivered?

What an encouragement to endurance and perseverance the predictive word can be to a church or individual as it inspires them to prepare their hearts and lives for the trials to come. This would seem to be the case with the word that was delivered to the church in Smyrna, according to Revelation 2:8–11. The church was told that it would suffer, some would be imprisoned and tribulation would be experienced for ten days, but the point of the message was, that the church should be faithful even unto death. How kind and loving of the Lord to reveal this so that the church may not fear, but prepare itself for the suffering to come. Prediction, therefore, is never an isolated declaration of news yet to happen. It is given for the specific purpose of causing the people of God to react in ways that they would not know how to, without having been given such knowledge. Prediction without motivating people to a course of action is not a biblical concept.

Strengthening

When the council at Jerusalem had made its decision
regarding the inclusion of Gentiles into the church and
that it was not required that they obey the entire law of
Moses: two prophets, Judas and Silas, went to the
church at Antioch to deliver the news. After the people
had received the news, it is recorded that Judas and
Silas stayed for a while at the church to encourage and
strengthen the brothers (Acts 15:30–32).

This aspect of prophetic ministry is also spoken of by
Paul, in 1 Corinthians 14:3, as being the result of the
exercising of the gift of prophecy to the church. Here he
points out that the effect of a prophetic word upon
individuals and/or the corporate body should be that of
strengthening, encouraging and comforting. The Greek
word for strengthening, *oikodome,* means to build up, to
make something strong. To encourage, in the New
Testament sense, means to revive a person's spirits, to
stir up, to strengthen them or give them hope. It is the
word *paraklesis* from which comes the word, Paraclete,
which is used of the Holy Spirit as our comforter/counsellor
(Jn. 14:15–18). The third word, comfort, which is closely
related to the second word, encouragement, means to
calm, pacify and especially to bring the comfort of love.
It is the word used of the Jews who brought comfort to
Mary and Martha at the death of Lazarus (John
11:19,31). The recipients of comfort in the New
Testament are, according to the *Theological Dictionary
of the New Testament* by Geoffrey W. Bromily
(Eerdmans/Paternoster, page 784), all those who sorrow,
the sick, prisoners, orphans and widows. What a wide
range of human needs is, therefore, ministered to when
a prophetic word is given.

These strengthening, encouraging, comforting words

are often simple and short. Consider Haggai's encouragement to the returned remnant at Jerusalem: 'I am with you, declares the Lord'. A simple, uncomplicated statement of truth, not elaborated upon, but coming with the very life and presence of God in the words. The result was that the previously discouraged people started building again. I will always be grateful to God that, in a meeting of a large church I was visiting as a member of the congregation, at the end of the service a complete stranger came up to me very apologetically and nervously and said: 'God says to you that he walks with you'. Little did he know the discouraging thoughts that had plagued my mind for a while, that were dispatched by that simple word. Prophetic people should not equate profundity with complexity, or effectiveness with the length of the prophecy. If they do, they will only create unnecessary pressure for themselves and probably take the edge off the words that they speak.

Where prophetic ministry has become silent in a church, the people often struggle with discouragement and with an unhelpful and unwholesome sense of weakness. At times, it moves from being a sense of weakness, to weakness itself. This is often seen in lethargy towards spiritual things, the struggle to trust, and even in our response to temptation, which then is more often to say yes than to say no to it.

When prophetic people are consistently moving in their gifting, then the church is strengthened and encouraged and the amount of counselling needed in these areas is greatly reduced. (This is not saying that there is no need for counselling, but that some counselling is rendered unnecessary by the consistent release of the prophetic word.) When teaching on the gift of prophecy, I always include a practical session in which people prophesy, under guidance, to one another. At the end of this time, I ask each individual whether what they received from another person by way of a prophetic word was relevant and helpful. Each time, nearly 100% of those asked, respond by saying that the prophetic word was relevant, encouraging and meaningful to them. This has been the experience of thousands throughout the world, that I have personally been involved with. This is one reason why I constantly encourage the regular use of the gift of prophecy in the church.

Strengthened people make for strong churches and strengthened churches make for strong people.

Presence

There is probably no greater experience to be had in worship than to be consciously aware of the presence of God. The sense of the immanence of God, in worship, is truly and wonderfully overwhelming as well as being awe-inspiring. Our response to such overwhelming experiential knowledge will vary, but one common response is literally to bow down before him. It is this experience that will ensure that, no matter how intimate a relationship we have with him, we will always be healthily aware that he is the Almighty and not the 'all matey'.

The gift of prophecy, when exercised by several different people (if not all those gathered) in a meeting, should, according to 1 Corinthians 14: 24–25, result in this awareness of God's presence, through the revelation, in a non-believer's heart and cause them to both fall down, and to confess that 'God is really among you'.

How wonderful to have the unbeliever, or one unlearned in the spirituals, to tell us that God is with us rather than the other way around. This is confession from an experience by the visitor, not an attempt at producing an experience from a convincing confession by us. Even more wonderful, is the fact that an unbeliever, in these circumstances, would acknowledge that they are a sinner and so repent and worship God. This is implied in the passage.

The silence of prophetic people who have become earthbound is often the reason why there is no sense or awareness of the presence of God in our meetings. Let us not confuse a meeting time that makes us feel good, with a meeting where there is the realised presence of God and/or the manifestation of the presence of God. The prophetic should move us from the acknowledgement of his omnipresence, through to the realised presence, and on to the experience of his manifest presence.

Some years ago, whilst I was attending a conference on the prophetic in Cardiff, two people ministered prophetically, making me so aware of God's presence that I fell on my face and did not dare open my eyes, for I felt that if I did, I would see him and that would mean my death. I had previously thought that I was clean before God, but when this happened, I could only lie prostrate and cry for mercy and forgiveness. It was as if a new standard of cleanness came alongside me that made mine appear grey (at best) in comparison. Talking with several others afterwards, I discovered that I had not been alone in the experience, for the conference hall had indeed become alive with the presence of God. I know people who have had the course of their ministry and their lives altered as a result of being in that meeting.

There is such a difference between intellectually knowing something and acknowledging it to be true, and being made so aware of the truth of something that it changes your whole outlook and being. Surely this is what lies behind the many references in Scripture that command us not to fear because the Lord is with us.

Such awareness of his presence makes the presence of fear incompatible with it.

What a privilege it is to have the prophetic moving amongst us bringing into our lives all that is in the heart of God for his people and what a void can result when it becomes silent.

NOTES
Prophetic Bulletin No.12 (Graham Perrins, 1991).
Used with permission.

Chapter 3

WHY EAGLES BECOME EARTHBOUND

There are many reasons why prophetic people stop receiving or giving prophetic words. It may be the result of their leadership's mishandling of the prophetic; because of the circumstances they have to cope with; because of tensions in their family relationships; or the result of people's reaction to words they have given in the past. This last reason we will deal with separately in the next chapter. Mixed in with all these factors are their own personalities and needs. They need to understand themselves as well as their circumstances if they are going to soar in the prophetic again.

Earthbound because of leadership mishandling

Most leaders of local churches do not deliberately set out to hurt or bind their prophetic people, but this often happens. When it does, the root cause is usually that the leadership does not understand prophetic people and their needs or know how to care for them properly. It is easy to frustrate them instead of fathering them, albeit unintentionally. The same applies to knowing how to administer the gift of prophecy in the corporate meeting. It is easy to end up policing the prophetic rather than pastoring it. Where this is the case, you often find prophetic people who are hurt, frustrated and earthbound.

As busy as local leaders are, they must make time (not simply try to find it) to get to know and understand their prophetic people. Failure to do this inevitably results in some or all of the following occurrences: 'off the wall' prophecies; an ongoing low level of content in the prophetic word; unhelpful reactionary words; a very irregular use of the gift of prophecy and a growing number of disillusioned prophetic people. Any of these will be to the detriment of the local church. Prophetic people need to know that they have access to leadership, not simply to pour out prophetic words to them, but to ensure that their prophetic ministry flows from a good relational base of understanding and care. Real relationships are of vital importance to all ministries and the prophetic is no exception. Now no one is perfect, and where this is not happening then the prophetic people must ask, in humility and understanding of the pressures on leaders, for such a caring relationship to be installed or rectified.

We must never assume that the local leaders know our desires and needs unless we tell them. This is being unrealistic. We must also be patient and not expect that everything will be put in order overnight. Neither must we settle for a quick fix, as was inferred by a speaker who I heard, saying, 'we are in a season of relationships in the church right now'. We are not talking of a season here; we are talking of an ongoing lifestyle in the local church. You do not 'do' relationships: you have them, nurture them and live them. This calls for time and it is an investment of time that will yield a high return in fruitful lives and fruitful ministry.

Prophetic people are often quite insecure in their inner lives and they need to be affirmed, or otherwise, when they have moved in their gift. Many a prophetic person has left a meeting still wondering whether or not they should have said what they did, or if they should have said it when they did. It is not good enough to adopt the attitude of one local leader, who said to me, 'If we do not say anything then they know their prophetic utterance was alright.' The leader may find this sufficient, but most prophetic people would not. Silence by leadership in such circumstances is definitely not golden. People deserve to know how their contribution has been received. The very opposite of silence in these situations is in fact like gold to the hearer: 'A word aptly spoken is like apples of Gold in settings of silver' (Prov. 25:11).

People need to be told either in the meeting, or privately afterwards that their word was acceptable, or not, as the case may be. To go silent on prophetic people is one of the worst things you can do as it fosters within them both uncertainty and insecurity. Conversely, we do not have to eulogise over every word they bring: a simple compliment or affirmation will suffice. There are times, of course, when it is unnecessary to say anything privately to the individual because the word they have brought publicly has been responded to publicly. If the word called for a response of some kind and the leadership followed this up by giving opportunity there in the meeting for the response, the prophetic person is neither left uncertain or insecure. It would do no harm, however, to still extend common courtesy to them afterwards and thank them for their faithfulness to God and his people by being obedient and speaking forth. As Gerald Coates, the Director of the Pioneer network of churches, often said to me, 'It is impossible to live under constant disapproval'. I would add that, for prophetic people, it is impossible to live under constant uncertainty as to whether or not their contribution was acceptable.

Another source of leadership mishandling is when prophetic people are caricatured by reference to them being strange, weird etc. How often we hear it said of someone either sarcastically or as a slur: 'Well they are prophetic!' as if this accounts for any unusual trait or occurrence. When people directly, or by inference, hear this often enough then the gift gradually becomes dormant. The reason for this is that they begin to believe what they hear and no one wants to be thought of as odd. Again, it is simply not good enough to say that they should rise above this. Most would love to, and probably could if it was only a matter of the conscious mind, but constant negative or derogatory speech will eventually find its way into the unconscious mind and there begin to affect the way one feels and acts. Such remarks do not always have to be addressed directly to the person in order to do damage: damage is caused to prophetic people when these remarks are heard regularly in ordinary conversation or in preaching.

To be prophetic is not synonymous with being strange, even if some biblical prophets did do strange things. All leaders would do well to see to it that their people (all of them) are constantly positively encouraged. If leaders want to see prophetic people blossom and, as a result, the church blossom, then they need to become, like Barnabas, sons of encouragement. I have tried to make it a practice to always specifically encourage anyone who has brought a prophetic word in any meeting I have been in. In my own church, even if a person needed some correction following what they said, I would always thank them for having the courage to step out in faith. Leaders should never think silence equals encouragement – it never does.

Besides the statements made about being strange etc, prophetic people are often labelled or referred to as emotional. We hear it said: 'Oh they are emotional you know', as if the person is suffering from a disease. To have and express emotions is not something that came into being as a result of the fall of man. Human emotions are a part of God's design for all mankind. Prophetic people, by nature, experience strong emotions: Elijah experienced depression; Jeremiah cried a lot both in public and private; Moses had his outbursts and David exhibited the whole range of emotions, as is recorded in the book of Psalms. Even Jesus, when delivering his prophetic word over Jerusalem did so with tears in his eyes (Luke 19:41), as well as weeping at the tomb of Lazarus. Emotions are not wrong, either in prophetic people, or any other form of gifting or ministry. They are only wrong when they become the source of our living, instead of a response to our living. For example, if I believe God loves me because I feel something, and question his love for me if I do not feel anything: then that is wrong. If, however, I feel exuberant or joyful, or if I feel overwhelming love because his word tells me that he loves me unconditionally and I believe it: then there is nothing wrong. This is living according to every word that proceeds from the mouth of God and experiencing emotion as a result, instead of allowing my emotions or lack of them to determine what is true. The 'stiff upper lip' of the British is certainly not biblical, neither is it helpful to being a well-adjusted person.

Leaders must also know how to administer the prophetic in their church. It is essential that every local church has a prophetic etiquette (or procedure) that is followed and that every member knows what it is and why the church has it. For example, the leaders may want every prophetic word to be referred to them in the meeting before being publicly given. They may arrange to have a point in the meeting where prophetic utterances are to be given. They may decide that all prophetic words must be given through the public address system. The New Testament is completely silent as to how you administer the prophetic, apart from the command of Paul in 1 Corinthians 14:29 that, after two or three prophetic words have been given they should be weighed by the congregation. Therefore, provided the leaders of a local church are not contravening any principle of Scripture, then however they decide to administer prophecy in that church is right for them. Having decided upon the way prophecy will be expressed in that church, the leaders should explain to the people exactly how it would work and the reasons why they have decided upon doing it that way. The bottom line for all of this is to remove areas of uncertainty that, otherwise, will hinder the flowing of the prophetic.

There is one final way in which prophetic people can be mishandled, which results in them becoming earthbound, and that is leaders who are insecure themselves. An insecure leader may feel threatened by the prophetic, unless the prophetic utterances are saying what he wants to hear, or what certain people in his church want to hear. If a leader is insecure, his insecurity can either turn him into a pleaser of people or a controller of people. When the prophetic words are not what the leader or certain people want to hear – because the words are not endorsing what is happening in their church, or because the words are saying something that the insecure leader has not thought of first – that leader may resort to trying to control the prophetic. This control will do damage to the prophetic and to the prophetic person.

Scripture has several examples of where leaders wanted to hear only those prophecies that pleased them and how they mistreated those who prophesied adversely. 2 Chronicles 18:4–27 is a striking example of this. Ahab, King of Israel, wanted Jehoshaphat, King of Judah, to join with him in attacking Ramoth Gilead. Jehoshaphat agreed, but wanted first to seek counsel of the Lord. Ahab brought four hundred false prophets together and asked them if he should go to war or not. 'Yes!' they all replied, assuring him of victory. This was what he wanted to hear. King Jehoshaphat, however, asked if there was a prophet of the Lord that they could ask. Ahab's reply speaks volumes: 'There is still one man through whom we can enquire of the Lord, but I hate him because he never prophesies anything good about me, but always bad. He is Micaiah son of Imlah' (v.7). Micaiah was called for and prophesied defeat. Ahab immediately says to Jehoshaphat: 'Didn't I tell you that he never prophesies anything good about me, but only bad?' (v.17). As a result, Ahab commands that Micaiah is put in prison and given a diet of only bread and water until Ahab returns safely – which he never did – for Ahab died in battle. Micaiah had made very plain in verse 13 that truth, not flattery or compliance, was what mattered in prophecy: 'As surely as the Lord lives, I can tell him only what my God says.' This was his reply when told to speak favourably to Ahab. This story is a clear picture of a leader being unable to handle a prophetic word that he did not like and the damage that he did to the prophet as a result. The following is a true story, as related to me, of how an insecure leader damaged the prophetic in his church:

I was once under a pastor who outwardly encouraged prophetic words in the congregation and allowed them to be spoken. However, when a member of the congregation did not like what was said, he/she would go to the pastor and complain. The pastor was a people-pleaser and would then try to manipulate the person who gave the prophetic word. He would claim that the prophecy was harsh and unloving, but would never give the person any specific reason why the word was harsh or unloving, but just made them feel condemned. Prophets are meant to be eagles, soaring high with God. Controlling them is similar to encouraging them to fly high, while placing a tether on their feet: the eagle takes off with great anticipation, but is suddenly jerked back to earth (control). After a while, the eagle becomes discouraged and gives up trying to fly.

Leaders must set a tone of positive encouragement for the prophetic in their church. I continually told my congregation that, in the exercising of the gift of prophecy, I gave them the right to make mistakes, provided they gave me the right to lovingly correct them if need be. The emphasis was placed upon lovingly correcting, not just correcting. It is so much easier to direct a moving car than a stationary one! As a result of the constant encouragement, we had a flow of prophetic contributions in the church and very rarely did we need to correct any. This was in contrast to another church, whose leader told his church that he would rather have one absolutely vital and correct prophecy than a number of mediocre ones. The result was that they never had a prophetic word in that church. The expectation was so high, that no one had the courage to bring a prophetic word. His desire for a profound and pure word became a discouragement to bringing any word at all.

In case anyone thinks I have been hard or unfair to leaders, let me say now that it was never my intention to be so. I have been a leader of one local church for over seventeen years and involved in leading churches for over twenty-five years and I know how difficult that can be. I honour the leaders of churches, but experience has shown that the above problems do arise, and unless we are aware of them, we will only exacerbate the problems of prophetic people.

Now, a word to prophetic people who have suffered as a result of the above mishandling or misunderstanding – do not wave this section under your leader's nose. Instead, forgive them, love and honour them. Pray regularly for them and, with God's help, put the incident or incidents firmly behind you. It is at this point that some prophetic people, because they are 'feelers' by nature, struggle with whether or not they have truly forgiven. They are often heard to say, 'but I don't feel forgiving', or else they say they have forgiven, but still feel extremely bad towards the person they have forgiven. In either case, they assume that they have not forgiven at all or that their forgiveness has somehow been incomplete. This problem occurs because of a wrong understanding of the nature of forgiveness. Forgiveness is an act of the will, not an emotional feeling. When someone chooses to forgive and does it, they have forgiven, regardless of what their emotions may feel. Bad and negative feelings towards a person do not negate the reality of their forgiveness of them. It is frequently the case that, having genuinely forgiven a person by an act of will, they find themselves struggling with adverse feelings towards the person for some time. This is because it takes time for emotions to catch up with where the will and spirit already are. To aid their emotions in this, they should pray positively for the person or persons they feel bad towards when those adverse emotions are making their presence felt. Rather than indulge their emotions for a while, they should ask God to bless the person, with health, spiritual growth, opportunities to serve and success etc. This will definitely shorten the time that it takes to feel genuinely positive about them. The following composite prayer will help settle this matter.

Lord Jesus, I have been hurt by the misunderstanding of (name the person). I will make no judgement of them as to their motive in this, or hold this against them. I forgive them completely and I ask you to forgive me for any wrongdoing or wrong attitude towards them. This is my will and desire and I believe before you that the matter of my forgiving is settled. I will not allow my emotions to cause me to doubt this. I now want to pray for them to be wonderfully used by you and blessed by you in everything that they are engaged in. Prosper them in all areas of their lives and continually do them good. Amen.

Earthbound because of the circumstances of our lives

Eagles mature more slowly than other birds. It takes them three to four years to reach adult plumage and, in the case of the golden eagle, some six to eight years. Most do not start to breed until they are about five years old. All of this points to the fact that maturity is not a quick process. It is the same for prophetic people. The circumstances of their lives are bound to their ministry. Life, for them, is God's training school, apart from any formal theological or Christian training they may have had or will receive. Therefore, the prophetic person will have to pass through a whole variety of life's experiences stretched over a lengthy period of time, in order to mature in their gifting. These circumstances can either make us signs to people portraying the prophetic word, or else the circumstances are used by God to bring about his purposes in our individual lives. The Apocryphal book Ecclesiasticus warns us of what to expect when serving the Lord:

> My, son if you come forward to serve the Lord, prepare yourself for temptation.
> Set your heart right and be steadfast, and do not be hasty in time of calamity.
> Cleave to him and do not depart, that you may be honoured at the end of your life.
> Accept whatever is brought upon you, and in changes that humble you be patient.
> For gold is tested in the fire, and acceptable men in the furnace of humiliation.
> Trust in him, and he will help you; make your ways straight, and hope in him.
>
> *Ecclesiasticus* 2:1–6 (RSV)

Moses' background as an Egyptian Prince in his early years and then on the run and spending forty years tending sheep in the desert, was all a part of his training for ministry in leading the children of Israel out of Egypt and through the wilderness. To Ezekiel, the Lord said, 'I have made you a sign to the house of Israel' (Ezek. 12:6,11). The loss of Ezekiel's wife and how he was to react to it, was part of his prophetic message to Israel. The same can be said of Hosea and his marriage, and Isaiah in naming his children. Their experiences in life were inextricably linked to their ministry.

The prophetic person will experience seasons in their

life when no revelation is being received because they are in the midst of circumstances that are designed to produce something in them or through them in the future. In the lives of Moses, Ezekiel, Hosea and David, personal tragedy seemed to be a part of their ministry. The personal histories of many prophetic people reveal severe trials that have been a major factor in their development. Judson Cornwall, in his book *Leaders Eat What You Serve* (Destiny Image, USA) puts it this way: 'When God calls a person to be a communicator for himself, he makes him a prophet, not a parrot. God more than speaks a word in the ear, he imparts truth in the inward parts. He makes his message become a part of his man, and then shares that man and the message with the people'.

At other times, the adverse circumstances in life can produce such stress and pressure that the prophetic person is incapable of hearing from God because their turmoil is, for them, making too much noise. I vividly experienced this at a church where the pastor is a good friend of mine. I had been invited to go there and form part of a prophetic team that would minister to participants in a school of prophecy run by the church. Arriving early, I spent time with the pastor before going with him to the meeting. Knowing I was going through a difficult time at my home church, he asked me how it was all going. While telling him of the difficulties and stresses I was experiencing, my spirit became agitated, as adverse emotions arose within me at the thought of the situation. Then it was time to go into the meeting. Almost immediately, some of the other members of the team started bringing words of prophecy and calling for a response. As people responded, I found myself being directed to minister prophetically both to the responding individuals and to the rest of the congregation. There was no time for me to calm my spirit, but I knew that unless I did, I would not hear God. Then I put myself under pressure as I thought, 'I must get a word'. Realising this was counterproductive to ministry, I asked to be excused from the meeting and drove home.

Then there are those well meaning people who put us under pressure to minister and instead of being able to, we find ourselves void of anything to say. I remember being part of a team invited to minister at a conference in India. Having introduced me to the delegates, the leader said to me: 'Please feel free to bring a prophetic word at any time'. The first meeting went extremely well, but I had nothing to bring. In each subsequent session, the conference leader repeated that I should be free to prophesy. The inference, seemed to be: 'This is what you came here for; please do it'. Soon, I was under pressure to bring something and, of course, that made it very difficult, even impossible, to receive a prophetic word. The prophetic simply shut down on me or, perhaps more accurately, my state ensured that I shut down on the prophetic! In any case, the prophetic is not like a tap that can be turned on at will: we can only listen. But if, through circumstances within and without our lives, that listening is defective, we will find it hard at best, and impossible at worst, to hear. It is also true that even when we listen with acute spiritual hearing, if God in his wisdom and sovereignty does not speak, then we have nothing to share either. Prophecy never originates in the will of man, but is always a revelation from God (2 Pet. 1:20–21).

We must learn, however, to differentiate between circumstances (both adverse and conducive) in our lives that God is using to teach us something that we will subsequently pass on to the body of Christ as prophecy, and those which belong to our own personal lives that do not warrant any wider spoken application. There is no formula in the Bible for determining this. Our intimate relationship with the Lord Jesus alone will enable us to hear him share whether or not the circumstances are purely for personal benefit or part of a prophetic message or sign to others. Prophetic people will search in vain for any kind of formula or keys in the Scriptures. God has ordained that they live out of their relationship with him and nothing is allowed to replace that. Elijah made that very clear when he introduced himself to King Ahab as one who stood before the Lord (1 Kgs. 17:1, KJV).[1] When we are uncertain as to whether these circumstances are solely for us or for us and others: the uncertainty, as well as the stress produced, will tend to keep us earthbound.

Earthbound because of family tensions

There is probably no other area that so adversely affects the effectiveness of our ministry than that of our family relationships. If we cannot love our family, how can we love the church? If we cannot love our family whom we see, how can we love God whom we cannot see? It is more likely that we will experience tensions in the family, than a lack of love for the family.

Tension in the family will inevitably spill over into our ministry and, as we have noted, tensions and pressures in the life of the prophetic person are counterproductive to effective ministry. Abraham, who is called a prophet by God (Gen. 20:7) experienced family pressure. God had given him the promise of a son and heir but as time went by and Sarai his wife did not conceive, she suggested to Abraham that a way of fulfilling God's promise would be for Abraham to sleep with her handmaid Hagar. This pressure resulted in Abraham being unable to make a quality decision to continue to trust that God would fulfil his word through Sarai. Instead, he slept with Hagar. As a result, Ishmael was born, and ultimately trouble ensued. Our ministry will never suffer as a result of our giving time to our families in order to minimise and prevent tensions occurring therein.

The causes of tension in families are many and varied, but there are four causes that do appear as common hindrances in the ministry of the prophetic person. Each one of these reasons merits a book, or at least a chapter, in its own right. Our purpose in this book is not to deal in depth with the causes, but to make one aware of them in order that more specific follow-up can be initiated if need be. The four reasons are:

1. Lack of a mutual sense of call between the prophet and their spouse

Primarily this will affect those prophetic people who are engaged in the ministry full-time, or considering it. This does not mean that your spouse has to have a prophetic ministry as well as you. It does mean that your spouse must have a realisation that their call is complementary to yours and vice versa. It means that you are in this together. Without this understanding, times will arise when, instead of a harmonious pulling together, it will seem as if those concerned are pulling in different directions. This will have a disastrous effect on any ministry, as well as the marriage itself.

2. Lack of quality time given to the family

We must watch out that we do not become so busy in our ministry that we have little time left for our family. Putting the Lord first in our lives is not synonymous with putting our ministry first. Our families are our first ministry responsibility, and that means ministering to the whole person not just to their spiritual needs. We need to give them time in leisure pursuits and normal family chatter. We have all heard the story of the wife who rang her husband up to make an appointment to see him. Unfortunately, such stories are not all fictitious: I have met couples where this has actually happened. To order and prioritise a busy diary is not easy, but it is essential if we are going to maintain a flow of the prophetic in our lives.

3. Lack of harmony in our lifestyle

Tensions will arise if we have different value systems relating to money, meetings, ministry, and possessions. Time spent in discussing these with each other will reap rich rewards for us. We cannot afford to ignore them, hoping that they somehow will resolve themselves. This never happens. Rather, the tensions caused by such become resentments and finally boil over into a full-scale problem.

4. Sexual frustration

When, for whatever reason, we cease making love with our spouse over an extended period of time, tension is created between us. Paul, in 1 Corinthians 7:5, exhorts the husband and wife not to deprive one another of sex, except by mutual consent, and then only for a specific time in order that they might devote themselves to prayer. Then, he says, they must come together again in order to avoid temptation. Sexual tension and frustration is a time bomb waiting to explode which, when it does, will destroy ministry.

Tensions in the family must be dealt with as soon as a person becomes aware of them. We must not be too proud to ask for help, if we are unable to resolve them ourselves. Pretending in front of others that all is well, when it is not, is a sure way of becoming earthbound at some point.

NOTES
[1]KJV (© Thomas Nelson, 1976)

Chapter 4

EARTHBOUND THROUGH PAST WORDS

At the beginning of the previous chapter, we said that one of the reasons why prophetic people become earthbound is because of the result or reaction to words given in the past. Words of prophecy that they had given in the past either did not come to pass, were inaccurate, or provoked a bad or adverse reaction in people.

No one likes to 'get it wrong'. However, we must realise that, whilst we are never to be irresponsible, we will never be infallible. (There is only one infallible person and he does not live in Rome!) We will all get it wrong sometimes, but that must not be allowed to stop us prophesying. There are clear ways in which we can deal with such occurrences and still retain our integrity, as well as credibility, for the ministry. Certainly prophetic people do not want their words to have an adverse effect upon the hearers: after all, part of the purpose of prophetic words is to build up and encourage the Body of Christ. Nevertheless, adverse reactions do occur. Once something like this happens, the tendency of the prophetic person is to close down their prophetic gift. Therefore, let us pause for a moment and look at these three occurrences: words not coming to pass, inaccurate words, and adverse response to words given.

Words that have not come to pass

When a prophetic word is predictive within a given time scale eg by this time next year, or in three months, and the time comes and goes without anything happening, then the best thing to do is to apologise to everyone concerned and say that you obviously got it wrong.

Some years ago, I prophesied about a new move of the Spirit that would take place in November of that year. I had – after sharing it with other brothers who, incidentally, could not say they believed it to be true but nevertheless encouraged me to give it out – prophesied this to a number of churches within our association of churches. The mentioned November came and went and no significant move of the Spirit occurred. Now there were some very kind and loving people who said to me that maybe it was because the churches did not pray enough. Again, some suggested that perhaps not enough faith was exercised, or that it all happened in the heavenly realm. I appreciated their attempts at trying to make me feel better, but the most honest thing was to admit that I was wrong. Consequently, via our association's newsletter, I wrote to all the churches in the movement, apologised, and repented for giving a word that clearly did not happen. The result of this action did not close any doors to me or cause people to say, 'Don't listen to him he gets it wrong'. Rather, people said what a blessing it was to hear reality spoken, instead of spiritual gymnastics being exercised in order to save face. I did not have any intention of misleading people or any desire to be wrong;

but it happened. I then faced a choice: whether to stop as a result of this or go on. One factor in choosing to go on, was the fact that I could look back over many words both predictive and otherwise that had come to pass and had been a source of blessing to the recipients.

In virtually every other realm of life, people don't give up when they make a mistake, so why treat the prophetic as different. As someone once said: 'The person who never made a mistake never made anything'. We can learn as much from our mistakes as from our successes.

It is relatively easy to determine whether or not a prophetic word has been fulfilled when a specific time for its fulfilment, or some other tangible means of assessing it, has been given. What do we do when the time-frame and other measurable criteria are not given? For example, suppose the following was prophesied: 'This church will double its size and new premises will become available for purchase requiring a step of faith'. Here, there is no indication of how long it will take or when these events will come to pass. How can such a word be judged? How long should the church continue to pray and exercise faith, and when should it give up, concluding that it was a wrong word. This can be a very difficult decision in practice. What is the answer in these and similar situations?

Paul, writing to the Corinthians, in 1 Corinthians 2:16, reminds them that, 'we have the mind of Christ'. Therefore, after the church and its leadership agree that a reasonable amount of time has elapsed relating to the prophecy, they should all meet together to seek the Lord and to enquire as to his mind in the situation. When he reveals his mind to the church, which he will surely do, then the appropriate action can be taken. In the context of the verse quoted above, Paul is very specific in pointing out that those who have the mind of Christ are those who are truly 'spiritual' and whose behaviour does not betray that fact. It is something that we also must take into consideration when calling people together to seek the Lord and to come to a conclusion.

It is also necessary to note that in the New Testament, the words spoken by way of the gift of prophecy are not so much written in stone and, therefore, a guarantee, as they are an invitation to co-operate with the Lord in them. That is why prayer, faith and perseverance are required for most prophetic words to be fulfilled.

Whilst writing this book, I received a letter from a man who, eighteen years ago, I had called out from the congregation in a church I was ministering in and prophesied over. He said that, while he had held on to the prophecy over that time period, nothing had ever happened to suggest that it would be fulfilled. Then, just recently, a series of events had occurred in his life and, after eighteen years, the prophecy had come true. To be honest, I had forgotten all about it and if I had been reminded of it, I would probably have said that I got it wrong. Therefore, we must be careful when dealing with situations like this and even more careful with the way we deal with the prophetic person responsible.

We know that many of the prophets in Scripture prophesied of people and events far in advance, but why should this happen in the contemporary gift of prophecy? Perhaps the main reason is, in order to keep us seeking God. The state of our heart may need to be changed as a condition of the prophecy being fulfilled and the prophetic word becomes like a promise that, kept before us, enables us to submit to the dealings of God as he works upon the condition of our heart.

One factor we have not spoken of is the witness or affirmation of the Holy Spirit to our spirit that this word is for us and comes from God. When this happens, then we must hold on to the word in prayer and watch its fulfilment at the 'proper time' (Luke 1:20). This is what the man in the aforementioned story did, even to my shame.

Inaccurate words

At first, this may seem to be identical with the last section. After all, is not a word that is not fulfilled inaccurate? This is true, but there are words that are not predictive, which are, nonetheless, inaccurate. For example, a church may be told that they are struggling and then given the reason why, when the truth is, they are not struggling and the so called explanation as to why is known to be irrelevant. This type is inaccurate, although there is no predictive element regarding the future in it. In this section, we will include all types of inaccurate words: the predictive that do not occur; the details that are incorrect; and the inaccurate, like the example above.

Now all prophetic people can, and probably will, give an inaccurate word or words at some stage in their ministry. When this happens, they will almost certainly begin to become earthbound. The reason for this is often a failure to understand the difference between inaccurate prophecy and false prophecy. No one wants to be known or classified as a false prophet. Prophetic people do not want to be responsible for deceiving the people of God. So, when there is no differentiation made between the inaccurate and the false in prophecy, God's eagles become earthbound.

We need, therefore, to see what constitutes a false prophet in the Bible. The two main passages that people use to maintain that one inaccurate word makes the giver a 'false prophet' are Deuteronomy 13 and 18. Is this what those passages teach, or not? We must give them closer attention.

The background to these passages is that Moses is preparing the children of Israel for entry into the Promised Land. That land would be found to be full of idolatry and Israel, in contrast, was to be faithful to *Yaweh,* the one true God. Inevitably, therefore, conflict would arise between those nations and the nation of Israel. Moses, knowing how Israel, in the past, had succumbed to idolatry by making the golden calf and had been deceived by Balaam, the false prophet, to commit sin, now in Deuteronomy 13 and 18 teaches them how to recognise false prophets.

The first thing he teaches them is that they must not be taken in simply by signs and wonders (Deut. 13:1–3). Here, the false prophet gives a sign that comes to pass, but says, 'Let us follow other gods . . . and let us worship them'. Here the test is not accuracy, but idolatry. If a word was designed to take people's hearts away from the Lord, then they were not to listen to or heed the words of the prophet. That is why Balaam was a false prophet. The issue was, what was the person ministering. Was it drawing people after God, to love him with all their heart, mind, and strength, or was it subtly, if not overtly, taking their eyes from him and setting their paths in a direction away from him? That is why the punishment of a false prophet was so severe in that it demanded the death penalty. 'That prophet or dreamer must be put to death, because he preached rebellion against the Lord your God' (Deut. 13:5). Note, he does not deserve death for a mistake, but for rebellion against God.

In the book of Revelation, when Jesus (via John) is addressing the church at Thyatira (Rev. 2:18–29), he condemns them because they tolerate a woman called Jezebel, who calls herself a prophetess, but leads his servants into sexual immorality and the eating of food sacrificed to idols. What is more, he promises that unless she and her followers (children) repent, then he will bring upon them intense suffering and even death. This is in complete harmony with Moses' teaching, as the desired end, both for the children of Israel and the church, is that evil and idolatry are purged from their midst.

When we come to chapter 18 of Deuteronomy, verses 14–22, Moses deals with a word spoken by a prophet that does not come to pass. It is totally inaccurate and the prophet is proclaimed to be false. Once more, the context is that of the idolatry and occultism of the nations living in the Promised Land, and Israel's command to follow only the Lord their God (Deut. 18:9–15). In verses 20–22, Moses speaks of three things that constitute a false prophet:

1. The false prophet speaks presumptuously

The word translated *presumptuously* means pride or arrogance and is used in Deuteronomy 17:12–13 in the sense of contempt, as well as a root word, rebellion, being used in Deuteronomy 1:43. It describes active rebellion to the will of God.

Another thought develops in Jeremiah of false prophets being those whose words had no origin other than their own imaginations (see Jer. 23:21–25). The trouble with their imaginations was that they were formed and influenced by the evil and ungodly character of their lives (verses 9–24).

In all these Scriptures, falsehood is tied to evil character and practices, not to an inaccurate word. In view of this, it is very important that prophetic people keep a watchful guard on their imaginations. With television programmes and advertisements, magazines, the internet and advertising in general, featuring sensual and sexual images, it is too easy for one's imagination to be turned towards impurity. The apostle Paul's command in Philippians 4:8 is especially relevant in this matter: 'Finally, brothers, whatever is true, whatever is noble, whatever is right, whatever is pure, whatever is lovely, whatever is admirable – if anything is excellent or praiseworthy – think about such things'. Obeying such a command will ensure that the imagination, the 'television screen' of the soul is kept clean and clear.

2. The false prophet has a demonic element in their prophecies

Moses taught of the prophet who speaks in the name of other gods (Deut. 18:20). We see in Deuteronomy 13:2,6,13, how the false prophet's goal is to turn people from God to worship idols. Jeremiah speaks of prophets leading Israel astray through prophesying by Baal (Jer. 23:13). At the church of Thyatira mentioned in Revelation 2:18–29, Jesus says that those who followed Jezebel's teaching were being drawn into Satan's so called 'deep secrets'.

Note that in these Scriptures the important point being stressed is the motivation behind the prophet and the goal of the prophet, not the literal accuracy of the prophet.

3. The false prophet speaks that which does not come to pass

Graham Perrins helpfully points out, in *Prophetic Bulletin* No.14, that the phrase 'does not take place or come true' (Deut. 18:22) can be translated 'the word is not'. He goes on to say, 'It lacks substance.

God's word has substance. It will not return void or empty, but will accomplish the purpose for which it has been sent.[1] This is not just a case of inaccurate prophecy, but of presumptuous (arrogant, rebellious) prophecy. This test of 'coming to pass' cannot be applied in isolation. It is part of a threefold description of a false prophet, which is not a pretty picture.

The understanding that false prophecy is not to be equated simply with inaccurate words of prophecy is in complete harmony with the teaching of both Jesus and Peter in the New Testament. Towards the end of the sermon on the mount Jesus, in Matthew 7:15–23, gives a warning about false prophets. In these verses, nothing is said about accuracy, but everything is to do with character. Hence, in verse 15, as Jesus commences his warning about false prophets, he says that there is a discrepancy between their outward behaviour and their inner life: their motives, attitudes etc. Outwardly, they look like sheep but inwardly are ferocious wolves. They know they are putting on an act in order to ravage the flock. How can we though, judge a person's inner life? The answer Jesus gives in verse 16 is, 'By their fruit you will know them' and he repeats this in verse 20. The context of verses 16 and 20 clearly refers to the outward fruit of character and actions and cannot be squeezed to imply that the fruit is that of being accurate or inaccurate. To remove all doubt about this, Jesus makes it crystal clear in verses 21–23 that the ability to prophesy does not of its self impress him. This is true even if the prophecies are one hundred percent true. The real issue is that of doing the Father's will: of aligning our lives with the revealed will of God in the Scriptures.

In 2 Peter 1:19–2:3, Peter, in speaking of the word of the prophets made certain and of the divine origin of prophecy, as against prophecy originating in the will of man, goes on to say in chapter 2 verse 1: 'But there were also false prophets among the people, just as there will be false teachers among you'. Here, by implication, Peter is saying that the marks of a false teacher (which he lists in verses 1–3) are the same as those of a false prophet. What, then, are those distinguishing marks?

a) 'Secretly introducing destructive heresies that deny the sovereign Lord who bought them' (v.1). In other words, like the false prophets of the Old Testament, they are taking people's hearts and minds away from following the Lord in truth.

b) 'In their greed these teachers will exploit you with stories they have made up' (v.3). Here, once more, the problem is the false teacher's inner life. Greed motivates them, exploitation of others is their goal, and dishonesty is their means of achievement: for they make up stories.

Would we call a teacher who makes a theological inaccuracy in a sermon a false teacher based on that inaccuracy alone? I do not believe we would; neither would we suggest that they stop preaching for a while as some sort of discipline. Old and New Testament evidence of a false prophet is clearly rooted into their character and inner life, for it is from this that their mouths speak.

In fact, some true prophets spoke words that were not fulfilled (Jonah 3:4–9). When Jonah prophesied judgement, he did not speak of a condition, such as repentance, that would avert it. He pronounced unconditional judgement and then became angry with God because God had mercy when Nineveh repented. It made Jonah look silly. Now we know, from the end of the story, that Jonah was aware that if the Ninevites repented the character of God was such that they would be forgiven. However, at the point of delivery of his prophecy, this was not mentioned at all and if we had applied our strict criteria of accuracy at that time, then the prophecy, clearly, was not fulfilled.

Ezekiel, in chapter 26 verses 7–14, prophesies things of Nebuchadnezzar that, if we compare with 29:17–20, were not accurate. Ezekiel says that King Nebuchadnezzar would come against the city of Tyre and ransack it completely, making spoil of the riches and merchandise. Now Tyre consisted of a main coastal city and an insular city on an island just off the coast. After a siege of thirteen years, Nebuchadnezzar conquered the mainland city, but not the island city, and he never received the spoil. In fact, the spoil that he did receive came from Egypt (Ezek. 29:17–20). The *Westminster Dictionary of the Bible* says that we cannot be certain that Nebuchadnezzar ever captured any part of the two cities. The island city fell to Alexander the Great, 240 years later.

Then there is the prophecy of Agabus in the New Testament (Acts 21:10–14), relating to Paul's arrest and subsequent imprisonment in Jerusalem. This prophecy contains two inaccuracies:

a) That the Jews would bind Paul, when Luke says the Romans bound him (21:33)

b) That the Jews would deliver Paul into the hands of the Gentiles, whereas, in fact, the Romans rescued him from death at the hands of the Jews (Acts 21:32–33).

Are we to conclude that these biblical prophets were false and deserved death? Certainly not. There is a lot more to being a false prophet than simply being inaccurate on the odd occasion.

Whilst Agabus may not have been strictly literally correct, nevertheless, the 'spirit' of the prophecy was correct. Again, as Graham Perrins says, in *Prophetic Bulletin* No. 14, 'The issue Moses is dealing with is not inerrancy, but idolatry'.[2]

I am fully aware that the above examples can be viewed and explained from positions other than mine, and so I assure my readers that none of the above should be seen as me 'having a go' at Scripture. I hold a high view of the Bible, believing it to be the infallible and inspired word of God

Cheer up earthbound eagles, you are not false, neither are you disqualified by inaccuracy. This is not to say that we can be irresponsible about accuracy, but it does mean that inaccuracy must not be allowed to damage the prophetic person who is seeking to bless the church and to be faithful to the Lord. Inaccuracy should provoke you to seek after the Lord with all your heart, constantly draw closer to him and, at his command, soar again.

Adverse response to words given

Adverse responses can come from individuals, leadership, or the corporate body. Such responses include: sarcastic remarks, rejection, silence, anger, misrepresentation and even blame. Rejection of a prophetic word can be particularly difficult to cope with. It will, however, help us if we keep in mind that Jesus also experienced a time when his words were rejected (Matt. 13:53–58). In this instance, familiarity bred contempt and they saw him as just a carpenter instead of the Messiah. There are times in our own lives when people are so used to us, they no longer listen and sometimes they can only see our lives, instead of hearing our message. It is, therefore, incumbent upon us that we do not express, as a word from the Lord, something that arises from any particular hobbyhorse of ours. We also need to ensure that our character is not saying something opposite to our message.

Whatever kind of negative response the prophetic person receives, it will, if not dealt with correctly, result in that person becoming earthbound. That is, they will not consistently exercise their prophetic gift.

In order to correctly handle adverse responses we need to keep in mind the following:

All prophetic words must be weighed by others (1 Cor. 14:29)

This means that the onus of responsibility to decide whether or not an utterance is a genuine word from the Lord rests, not with the one bringing it, but with those to whom it is given ie the body. The gift of prophecy does not impose on the church its veracity – the church gives the word of prophecy its authentication. All prophetic people are in submission to the local church, as far as determining the veracity of the prophecy is concerned. This is why it is so important both to weigh prophetic words and to know how to weigh them properly. If we do not weigh, then we will not know what response to make and if we do not weigh correctly, then we may make a wrong response. Paul, in 1 Thessalonians 5:19–21, attributes the putting out of the Spirit's fire to treating prophecies with contempt (as of no account) and not testing them.

The word translated 'test' *(dokimazo)* in the above

passage, means: to examine, to see if genuine, as when examining metals. The word translated 'weigh' *(diakrino)* in 1 Corinthians 14:29 means: to distinguish, to evaluate. Putting the two together we can say that in weighing or testing a prophetic word we are to evaluate and examine by sifting the good from the bad and the helpful from the unhelpful. At the same time, we must look for that which is right, good and positive and put the emphasis there. This is what Paul means when, in the context of testing (1 Thess. 5:19–22), he says: 'Hold on to that which is good. Avoid every kind of evil.' The latter sentence is better understood as, 'avoid wrong of every kind'. This means that sometimes a prophetic word may be a mixture of that which is right and that which is wrong or inaccurate. When we hear such a word, we are not to write the whole thing off because of the wrong, but let go of the wrong and hold fast to that which is right. The church and the prophetic person will feel secure and helped if both parties know that the prophetic word has been correctly weighed. In weighing prophetic words, we need to ask ourselves a number of questions regarding the content, the messenger and the manner of the words. The following questions will help the church learn to weigh words correctly. They will even help the prophetic person discern before delivering a word the rightness, or otherwise, of that word.

1. Questions of content
● **Does it conform to Scripture?**
   This does not mean we have to find a chapter and verse to back up the prophetic word, but it does mean that the prophetic word must be in accord with the whole tenor of Scripture.

   I once heard a prophetic word being given to a congregation that began, 'The Lord says, you are a stench in his nostrils'. This word continued in much the same vein, piling condemnation upon condemnation onto the people of that church. Here was a clear example of a word being against the whole tenor of Scripture. How can our lives be hid with Christ in God and at the same time be a stench to God? Can we be clothed in the righteousness of Christ, acceptable to the Father and be regarded as repulsive to him? No, never! This is not to say a chastening word cannot be from the Lord, for clearly it can. The issue in the above example was that the words purporting to be from the Lord contravened what the Scriptures say is our standing and position before him, together with his view and acceptance of us. When God speaks a chastening word to his people, it will have a condition attached that, if his people respond to it, he will ensure that grace, mercy and restoration are available to them. However, in the above example there was no talk of anything other than a tirade of condemnation. This word was rightly weighed and found wanting because it did not conform to the tenor of Scripture.

- **Does it promote the knowledge of God (Eph. 1:17)?**
  The Holy Spirit, who gives revelation, gives it, according to this verse, in order that we might know God better: that we might have a more complete knowledge of him. Granted, this verse is speaking of the ministry of the Holy Spirit in the believer's life. Nevertheless, the Holy Spirit, being the author of all true prophecy, will likewise cause prophetic utterances to result in the increased knowledge of God. This knowledge is not designed to give us academic facts alone about God, but to promote a hunger and thirst for him that we might then declare him. Karl Barth once said that the point is not to speak 'about' God, but to speak 'from' him.

- **Does it strengthen, encourage and comfort (1 Cor. 14:3)?**
  A prophetic word need not contain all of these three elements but it should contain at least one of them.
- **If predictive or revelatory, is it accurate (Deut. 18: 21–22)?**
  See previous section on inaccurate prophecies
- **Does it draw us closer to God (Deut. 13:1–4)?**
  Even a disciplinary word should cause us to return to God, or to run after him. It should not have the effect of making us want to run from him. Words of affirmation should, likewise, cause us to draw nearer to him and not indulge in any form of self-congratulation.
- **Does it point us to Jesus (Rev. 19:10)?**
  The phrase 'spirit of prophecy' was a rabbinic phrase that meant Holy Spirit. That is, the Holy Spirit is the author of all true prophecy, which will bear witness to Jesus.

2. Questions of the messenger

- **Is the messenger solid stable and mature in their Christian life and of sound character (Matt.7:15)?**
- **Are they free of serious emotional and psychological problems? If not are they receiving help in these areas?**
- **Are they in good standing with the fellowship?**
  Unknown, wandering 'prophets' should not be allowed to address congregations, as this can cause untold problems. Neither should those members who have unresolved difficulties with the fellowship be let loose upon the people.
- **Are they free from wanting to control, manipulate or to have significance through their utterance?**
  Care needs to be exercised here, as we can easily attribute wrong motives to people. After all, only God

knows the true motives of a person's heart. However, we can be aware of a person's history in these matters. We must also be alert to the Holy Spirit creating uneasiness within us, which causes us to see in the message traits of control, manipulation or self-significance.

3. Question of manner
- **Is the prophecy delivered in a spirit of love?**
Jesus delivered his prophecy regarding the destruction of Jerusalem with tears in his eyes (Mat. 23:37). This is not to be confused with sentimentality, but should convey something of the compassionate nature of God.

Together with the aforementioned, it is also helpful to ask ourselves: 'What was the inner witness I experienced when the prophecy was delivered? Did I feel a rise of faith, or did I feel distinctly uneasy?' 1 John 2:27 says: 'the anointing you received from him remains in you, and you do not need anyone to teach you.' The context of this verse is about being led astray and knowing truth from error. It does not mean that the teaching ministry is now redundant. It means we have someone within us (the Holy Spirit) who lets us know when we hear something wrong: that what we are hearing is error. We may not be able to articulate the error, that is part of the job of the teaching ministry, but we are aware that all is not right.

It is not necessary that every prophetic word satisfies all of the aforementioned criteria but, where any of those criteria are found to be wanting, we must weigh the prophetic word accordingly. Once a prophetic word has been weighed, then not only should the result be communicated to the person bringing it, but also the criteria used for weighing it. It should be explained upon what basis the word was accepted, wholly or in part or rejected. This approach will certainly teach invaluable lessons to the giver of the prophetic word as well as helping them develop further.

Each individual bears moral responsibility for the decisions that they make

The prophetic person cannot be blamed for consequences that another person's decisions have caused, albeit in so-called response to the prophetic word. If the receivers of a prophetic word do not fulfil the conditions of that word, then the person bringing it cannot be blamed for the results or lack of results. Likewise, if a prophetic word is not prayed over in order to see it fulfilled, then the person giving it cannot be blamed for the non-fulfilment. The parable of the sower is a salutary lesson that however pure the word sown the final result depends upon the condition of the heart that receives it.

The person bringing the word of prophecy has responsibility to bring that word, not responsibility for ensuring that it is received or that it comes to pass

There is, of course, a responsibility to pray about the prophetic word once it has been given by the person who gave it. However, that responsibility is very different from them trying to make it happen.

All recipients of prophetic words, like those giving them, are human and fallible

They will not always respond as one would like or even hope for. Therefore, it is important to be forgiving and to ensure that a pure and clean heart is kept towards them. Like the prophetic person, the recipient of a prophetic word can also get it wrong in their response. Just as getting it wrong must not be aloud to bind us from exercising the gift, neither must a wrong response stop us or intimidate us from operating our prophetic gift.

As well as the above reasons for a prophetic person becoming earthbound, the prophetic person's own character needs and temperament traits may play a part in keeping them earthbound. Prophetic people seem to have certain common characteristics and traits which, when not recognised or fulfilled, can lead to the person not functioning. This will be the subject of our next chapter.

NOTES
[1]*Prophetic Bulletin,* Graham Perrins. Used with permission.

[2]*Prophetic Bulletin,* Graham Perrins. Used with permission.

Chapter 5

PRESSURES AND PAINS OF PROPHETIC EAGLES

As mentioned in the previous chapter, prophetic people do seem to have common temperament traits and needs, which can be both a pressure and a pain to them, as well as a means for great blessing.

If prophetic people are to be a source of great blessing in the church, then they need to be understood by others and they need to understand themselves. Misunderstanding by either, will result in them becoming earthbound eventually. It is always sad to see someone struggling with issues in their lives, without an understanding of why this is occurring or how they can deal with it. The purpose of this chapter is to show some of the common issues that adversely affect prophetic people and cause pressure and pain in their lives.

Frustration

This can be a major problem in the life of a prophetic person. Frustration causes an agitation of spirit that militates against hearing clearly from God. It also hinders our walk in holiness and our fellowship with others, as the tendency to explode, because of the frustration, is often given expression. Frustration can result, in the life of a prophetic person, when any of the following three things happen – unless that person understands how to handle the situation:

1. When something is obvious to them but not obvious to others
2. When they see but cannot say
3. When they cannot have the time to be quiet or alone.

Let us take each of the above circumstances and look at them in greater detail.

1. When something is obvious to them but not obvious to others

As mentioned previously, a prophetic person is a 'seer'. They, through their gifting, can see things that others cannot and sometimes, instead of realising that it is only obvious to them because of their gifting, they believe that everyone else should be able to see it as well. I have often heard such people say, 'it is obvious to anyone' or 'well it is only common sense'. In fact, nothing could be further from the truth. It is not obvious, neither is there common or natural sense involved, but, rather, revelation. The difficulty is that often, to the prophetic person, their gifting appears to be quite natural, whilst being observed as supernatural by others. Therefore, they become frustrated, for they expect others to see as rapidly as they do or as clearly as they do. When this happens they must understand that it takes time for other people to see or understand what they are seeing. Proclamation and patience need, so often, to be twin experiences in the life of a prophetic person. If (or when) they are tempted to cry: 'Why can't they see it yet?' 'How long is this going to take?' or 'If we wait much longer we will miss it', then it is definitely time to engage in serious prayer for understanding to be given to those who can't 'see'.

The prophetic person should not live in isolation from their word. They have a responsibility to either pray it into being or pray that it will not come to pass, as is appropriate. In Genesis 18:17–33, Abraham receives a word from God that he (God) is going to destroy Sodom and Gomorrah. Immediately, Abraham begins to pray that such an event will not take place. On this occasion though, the conditions that Abraham cites to request such mercy from God are not to be found in the lives of the two cities' populations. In the case of Moses, as recorded in Exodus 32:7–14, God told him that he would destroy the people of Israel, because of their return to idolatry by the making of the golden calf. Like Abraham before, Moses at once began to intercede on behalf of the people. This time, the Lord relented and saved the people from destruction. Jeremiah, when speaking of the false prophets (Jer. 27:18) says, 'If they are prophets and have the word of the Lord, let them plead with the Lord Almighty'.

Even the first mention of the word 'prophet' in the Bible (Gen. 20:7) links the prophet to prayer. The prophetic person cannot simply proclaim and forget, or proclaim and blame; they must be prepared to engage in prayer about their word. This will help relieve them of the feelings of frustration that may otherwise arise.

2. When they see but cannot say

A second cause of frustration for the prophetic person is when they see, but God says 'do not say'. In other words, do not speak of this that I am showing you, or proclaim it. The Apostle Paul, the Apostle John and also Daniel experienced this (2 Cor. 12:4, Rev. 10:4 and Dan. 12:4).

Why, you may ask, would God reveal something and then tell you not to share it? If we cannot answer this question, then indeed frustration can be the result. Some light can be shed upon our question by Adam Clarke's commentary on the verse from Daniel mentioned above.

Firstly, we see that it was a matter of timing. We must not assume that the moment of revelation is the time to pass it on. Timing is all-important in the giving of prophetic words. However, we can still ask the question: 'Why doesn't God leave the revelation until the time to give it?' Such a question makes two assumptions, neither of which is always valid. The first is that what we receive on any occasion is the complete picture of what God intends to reveal to us. Secondly, that all prophecy is a spontaneous thought and cannot be meditated upon in order to see if God wants to reveal more. Often a person will receive a word from the Lord that is like a first instalment of the whole word, the rest of which is yet to come. One might, then, ask: 'How do you know if there is more to be revealed or not?' There is no easy formula for knowing this, only a dependency upon our intimate relationship with the Lord. It is imperative that we ask him, if not overtly, then certainly by our attitude of listening to him, whether or not there is more to what we are seeing.

Secondly, there is the question of understanding. We

may receive something but not understand it at the moment. Our lack of understanding is not to be, in this case, an ultimate state of ignorance, but an inspiration to seek the Lord for further enlightenment. Such a seeking after God takes time, as is illustrated in Proverbs 25:2: 'It is the glory of God to conceal a matter; to search out a matter is the glory of kings'.

I have known of prophetic words being given that no one could understand the meaning of. It would have been better if the person sharing such a word had waited upon the Lord, seeking understanding. After all, the essence of a prophetic word, according to 1 Corinthians 14, is that it is understandable by the congregation. Again, as mentioned previously, there is also the matter of prayer. God sometimes gives revelation to people, not in order for them to share it publicly, but in order for them to intercede privately. How we all like publicity, and if the desire to be noticed or thought highly of has not been dealt with in our lives, then frustration will be the result of seeing something that must be held in private and prayed over.

3. When they cannot have the time to be quiet or alone

The third cause of frustration in a prophetic person happens when they cannot find the time to be quiet and/or alone with the Lord. Not all prophetic people are lovers of solitude or inveterate loners. Most of them enjoy the company of friends and others. They are also engaged in activities within and without the church, including jobs and vocations. However, it does seem that there is a common trait amongst them to have times of quiet and to be alone in the conscious awareness of the presence of God. This is not to say that Christians with other gifts and callings do not have these desires, but that these desires are particularly strong in prophetic people. It is when these desires are thwarted that frustration occurs.

It is very important for prophetic people to build into their diaries times for quietness and for being alone with God. We must remember that, in the mainly pastoral setting of the Old Testament, there was neither the noise nor the rush that we, in our time, experience every day. This noise and speed of life can have a very dulling effect upon our ability to hear the Lord, and if we know that we are not hearing prophetically like we used to, because of this, then frustration results: unless we deal with it.

Similarly, in the New Testament, people did not try to pack into their lives the amount that we do today. This was mainly because it took much longer to get anywhere than it does today, with our high-speed travel. It was considerably easier to be consciously listening to God whilst walking for days between towns and cities, or even riding at a leisurely pace upon a donkey, than it is for us in a car speeding up a motorway or stuck in a traffic jam!

Even Jesus, in his cultural setting, took time out to be alone with his father. To be a spiritual workaholic, even if it does not become frustrating, will not make for an effective prophetic ministry.

Recognition

The desire to be recognised can become a strong pressure in a prophetic person. Usually, such need for recognition finds expression in wanting a reputation or approval, and is often more subtle when our ministry becomes our identity. All Christians, whether prophetic or not need to have dealt/to deal with the inner need for a reputation and/or approval. The problem with the need for a reputation is that in the end it affects both our style and content. It can be seen at its worst when we recognise in another, a carbon copy image of a more mature and recognised prophetic ministry. As in every aspect of the Christian life, anointing and effectiveness do not result from copying others who are anointed and effective. It comes first from sovereign choice and second by responding to that choice by humbly walking with God. As always, relationship with him is far more important than ministry. Remember the words of Jesus in Matthew 7:21–23. Here, Jesus speaks of those who appear to be very successful. They have prophesied, driven out demons and worked many miracles in his name, yet he still says 'I never knew you. Away from me, you evildoers!' It is not just our initial relationship with him, through conversion, that is important, but our ongoing relationship with him. The greatest commandment, according to Jesus, is not, 'you shall *serve* the Lord your God' but, 'you shall *love* the Lord your God' and that love is to be with the whole of our being. Then comes the serving aspect, 'and your neighbour as yourself'.

One biblical character who was obviously not worried about his reputation was Elisha. In 2 Kings 5:8–19 we have the story of Naaman, commander of the army of Aram: valiant and highly respected by the King of Aram. However, Naaman was a leper. An Israelite girl had been taken captive and was now the servant girl to Naaman's wife. This servant girl told her mistress that if Naaman would see the prophet Elisha he would be healed of his leprosy. So it was that, eventually, Naaman came to be standing outside Elisha's door. What an opportunity for Elisha to make a name for himself and to gain favour and reputation with the Aramites. Even Naaman thought that Elisha would make a display before him, but what did Elisha do? He sent a messenger to Naaman with the words, 'Go, wash yourself seven times in the Jordan, and your flesh will be restored and you will be cleansed'. Naaman could not believe the treatment he received. Elisha certainly gained neither favour nor a favourable reputation at that moment. Naaman was furious and went away. Later after he had calmed down, had followed Elisha's instructions and had been healed completely, he returned to Elisha and wanted to give him a gift (a very considerable one at that, v.5), Elisha refused the gift, risking offending Naaman all over again.

Obviously, Elisha did not care about building or keeping a reputation. What was it that freed him from such a need? In a word: servanthood. He had learned this in his association with Elijah (2 Kgs 3:11). To embrace the true meaning of being a servant, and acting like it in the way we live, will release us from the desire for a reputation. This release in our lives will come as we constantly remind ourselves that we are servants of God and servants to the people he has given us to minister to. Jesus himself was the role model of true servanthood, as expressed in Philippians 2:7: Jesus 'made himself nothing, taking the very nature of a servant, being made in human likeness'. The King James Version says, 'He made himself of no reputation'. The idea expressed, is one of emptying. Jesus emptied himself of everything except his divine nature and came, not to be served, but to serve. We, his followers, should do likewise, beginning, perhaps, with a lessening emphasis upon being a leader or having a ministry and a greater emphasis upon being a servant.

Even when we have overcome or are overcoming the

pressure of wanting a reputation, we can find ourselves with an inordinate desire for approval. If this pressure remains with us, it will almost certainly lead us to say things which we think will gain us approval, rather than those things that need to be said because God has revealed them to us. This was a problem that some prophets of the Old Testament had. According to Alan Kreider, in *Journey Towards Holiness* (Marshall Pickering, page 96–99):[1] within a century, the roving bands of prophets in the time of King Saul had become part of the royal establishment and, from then on, prophesied what was acceptable to others, in contrast to the dissident prophets, who spoke unpopular words, but words that came by revelation from God. A striking example of this behaviour can be seen in the four hundred prophets falsely assuring King Ahab of God's blessing (which is what he wanted) and Ahab's reaction to the true words of the prophet Micaiah, of whom Ahab said, 'I hate him because he never prophesies anything good about me'. The same was true in Jeremiah's day. Hananiah prophesied good news to order, regarding the breaking of the yoke of the King of Babylon a decade before Nebuchadnezzar captured the city. Jeremiah, on the other hand, constantly warned Jerusalem of the coming judgement and, like Micaiah, ended up in prison as a result.

The Apostle Paul recognised that tension exists, between the need for approval and faithfulness to the Lord, in Christian service. He emphatically tells the Galatians that he will not please men, but only God. This is what he says in Galatians 1:10: 'Am I now trying to win the approval of men, or of God? Or am I trying to please men? If I were still trying to please men, I would not be a servant of Christ'.

How can the prophetic person ensure that the need for approval will not impinge upon their ministry, or be a constant drain on them as they battle to overcome it? It is helpful to recognise that the need for approval is often rooted in our basic insecurity. The more secure we are in Christ and in our relationship with him, the less insecure we will feel. The less insecure we are, the less will be our need for approval. The question that arises now is this: how can I be more secure in Christ?

Fundamentally, you cannot be more secure, because you are *absolutely* secure in him. What is needed is the experiential knowledge of that glorious truth and that comes through study and knowledge of the doctrine of being in Christ. The book of Proverbs says: 'As he thinketh in his heart so is he' (Prov. 23:7, KJV).[2] We need to be constantly meditating upon and believing the truth revealed in the written word of God about our acceptance in Christ, position in Christ, acceptance before God: recipients of his abounding love. None of these things are dependent upon our performance, but are solely dependent upon our position in him. It is not enough to simply hold these truths as a mental statement of faith: they must be a living part of us that truly affect the way we think and act. I believe that it is true to say that my intimate and experiential relationship with Jesus is the result of being grounded in the great doctrines of the Scriptures, which began soon after my conversion. Have I still felt the need for approval? Yes, and on many occasions. But I know what to do on those occasions: I recall truth and ask the Lord Jesus to make that truth live for me at the moment I need it. Along with that, I must confess that I also pray, 'and let me be aware of your presence just now.'

There is also an unwholesome way of coping with the

need for recognition, and that is when we make our ministry our identity. Being uncertain of our acceptance as a person by others, we retreat behind our gifting. Of course, we are uncertain of our acceptance by others because we have difficulty in accepting ourselves. This then becomes the unconscious motive for creating a ministry image that never lets us be known simply as an ordinary person.

I have a friend who has a powerful international prophetic ministry. This person was very difficult to get to know at a level beyond his prophetic ability. In time, he forgot how to be ordinary and was always in 'ministry mode'. After all, that is what he thought he was – a ministry. I remember being in a restaurant with him and some other friends who were also pastors. It was a day off for all of us, when we could relax and enjoy each other's company. The sad thing about my prophetic friend was that he could not switch off. Throughout the meal, and afterwards, he kept asking if any of us had a word from God, or whether certain numbers, words, phrases etc. were meaningful to us. We could never get to know anything about him other than what his ministry was. Tragically, some time later he had a nervous breakdown; but I am glad to say that, although it has taken some time, he is on his way to full recovery. This is an extreme case, but it does illustrate the pressure that can be experienced when we cannot let go of the ministry image. We must also make sure that we do not allow people to reinforce that image, and thereby make it difficult for us to be ourselves amongst them. Honesty, transparency and vulnerability before people will crucify the need for recognition, reputation and approval, and will, instead, create acceptance, identification and true friendship with them. Underline these words in your mind: *I am what I am, and I am of worth; not because of what I do, but* because *I am in Christ, who has caused me to be unconditionally loved by my heavenly father. And so I have been saved, am being saved and will yet be saved.* Oh the wonder of liberating truth!

Barren periods

There are times in the prophetic person's life, when it seems that, for no apparent reason, words of prophecy or revelatory facts and insights are not given. At such times, seeking the Lord and trying hard to be receptive does not cause the prophetic to spring forth. These periods can be very difficult to live through. Thoughts like 'I have lost my way, my anointing, or my ministry' bombard our minds, together with other thoughts such as, 'I must have done something wrong', or 'God is punishing me'. Whilst any of the above thoughts, if true, would result in a barren period; usually barren periods are not the result of any of these things happening in a person's life. If we look at the lives of prophetic people in the Bible and consider how little is said by them, compared to the length of their lives, then we realise that it is normal for the prophetic to ebb and flow. There were very long periods in the life of Elijah, for example, when we have no idea of what he was up to. There are seasons in the prophetic of intense activity and there are seasons of no activity: both are normal. As Graham Cooke says, God does not always speak initially, but he always speaks eventually. The trouble is, the length of time that lapses before it eventually happens. Because we have believed that a truly prophetic person will have a constant flow of prophetic words, we struggle when the flow stops. The worst thing we can do, when in a barren period, is to panic or allow our confusion to bring on depression. Barren periods do not necessarily say anything about the state of our relationship with the Lord, nor do they provide a guiding assessment of his thoughts towards us. More often than not, they are simply the normal experience of a prophetic person's life. I can remember a period of eighteen months in my life when I could not receive any fresh word from the Lord. I could not even prepare a new sermon during this time. In spite of what I knew about the ebb and flow of the prophetic, I was convinced that for some unknown reason God had abandoned me in this area. Then, I was asked to spend three months in America, at Christian Fellowship of Columbia. The first Sunday I walked into the building, revelatory words just came into my mind one after another. I had not become a different person, I had not done anything different, but the barren period was over. My wife said to me after the meeting, and again during the next three months that we were resident there: 'You are flying again'. Indeed I was, and it felt good again; but what was the reason or cause of the barren eighteen months? I still do not know, other than the fact that it happened. Did I learn anything from the experience? The only thing I came to realise was this: I do not own the ministry; the Lord of the ministry owns me.

There is another reason why we experience barren periods: because of spiritual attack. I must confess that, in my eagerness not to attribute every adverse circumstance to the Devil's harassment of my life and thereby give undue attention to him, I am sometimes slow to recognise when he is, in fact, launching an attack upon me. As I said in Chapter 1, Satan hates the church and hates the individual believer. He is not some embittered old man who dislikes us. He is the consummate evil one who is unsurpassed in his hatred of God and all that is good, righteous, pure, and holy. He is committed to bringing us down and stopping the Kingdom of God advancing. His intense hatred of us, the people of God, is fuelled by the fact that the very thing he coveted, ie the throne of God, and could never have, has been made available for us to share as the bride of Christ (Rev. 3:21). Fortunately, he has lost the war and will never succeed in his evil desires because of the victory of our Lord Jesus Christ upon the cross and his resurrection from the dead.

All of this does not mean, however, that we will not at times be subject to one of Satan's onslaughts, but it does mean that we do not ultimately fail. Remember when Jesus addressed Simon Peter, saying: 'Simon, Simon, Satan has asked to sift you as wheat'. Jesus added, 'But I have prayed for you, Simon, that your faith may not fail' (Luke 22:31–32). By this, Jesus guaranteed Peter would make it. Not by his strength or by any other means at Peter's disposal, but by the commitment of the Son of God to him. That same Jesus, 'Who always lives to intercede' for us (Heb. 7:25). Peter's faith did temporarily let him down, but it did not ultimately fail: and that is what Jesus promised. Therefore, we need not fear that any barren period caused by spiritual attack will result in the permanent loss of our ability to move in the prophetic in the future.

Spiritual attacks can come to us in many forms, just as they did to people in the Bible. Elijah is a prime example of this. In 1 Kings 19:1–18, the story is told of Jezebel launching an attack upon Elijah that so filled him with fear that he wanted to die. Moreover, his fear led him to experience a barren period of forty days as he went on the run from Jezebel. In between an angel coming to him and God speaking to him, Elijah heard and saw nothing for those forty days. This attack was more than the expressed temper of Jezebel: it was a direct demonic attack, which came in the guise of Jezebel. It came because Elijah had called Israel to return to following the Lord God and to forsake following the religion of Baal (1 Kgs. 18:21). Elijah threw down the gauntlet against the prophets of Baal and Asherah, and that included Jezebel. Jezebel had sought to suppress the worship of Yahweh by killing off the Lord's prophets (1 Kgs. 18:4) and she was personally involved with 850 prophets of Baal and Asherah, openly showing them favour (1 Kgs. 18:19). According to the Old and New Testaments, behind the literal idols of the nations, there lie demonic spirits (Ps. 106:36–37; 1 Cor. 10:20–21). Therefore, there was demonic inspiration behind Jezebel's anger, which was expressed in her death threat to Elijah (1 Kings 19:1). Now one would have thought that if you were going to kill someone you would not announce it to them in advance, as Jezebel did. Why did she take such action? Clearly, her death threat was no idle threat, but she wanted something else as well and that was to bring Elijah into abject fear before the threat was carried out. She knew that if she could cause Elijah to be dominated by fear, then it would stop him from ministering for the period between her threat and the actual carrying out of it. In other words, she would be both temporarily and ultimately successful in preventing his prophetic ministry being exercised. In instilling fear, she was temporarily successful, but she completely failed in her proposed course of action. Instead of Elijah being killed, God caused Elijah to triumph, while Jezebel suffered the very fate that she had planned for Elijah.

In barren times, fear is often the number one tactic of the enemy. When the Devil causes a prophetic person to have a barren period, as in the case of Elijah, it can lead them into total despair (1 Kgs. 19:4). When attacks like this come upon us, we must remember that we will be victorious in the end, because we have the totally victorious one interceding for us. Along with this, we must also believe that, because of his mercy and love, we will again hear from him and have an encounter with him, just as Elijah did after the forty days (1 Kgs. 19:9–15).

I would like to be very open at this point with you, the reader, and share my testimony of a barren period. It happened during the summer of 1998. For many months I had not been able to receive any fresh word from the Lord: I could not even prepare a new sermon and I was under intense pressure on every side. It seemed as if a black hole had swallowed me up and nothing I did or tried alleviated it. Having, for most of my life, felt the presence of God, I now found that even that was a thing of the past. I was living, it seemed, only on auto-pilot.

One morning, in despair, I walked along the beach of my home town intending to pray, but the heavens were as brass. I was in severe financial straits and no matter how much I quoted and pleaded the verse, 'my God will meet all your needs' (Phil. 4:19), no provision had been forthcoming. Emotionally, I felt abandoned and considered just walking out into the sea and ending it all. I am ashamed to say that the only reason that I did not do so was that I was afraid of drowning. So, in total despair and depression I sat on a breakwater and cried. Then, for the first time in months, I became aware of the presence of God. The whole beach seemed alive with his presence. He did not say anything to me, but right there he took my utter despair away and I began to walk out of the black hole. I was reminded of when our fourteen-year-old daughter had been rushed into hospital with severe abdominal pains. We had given consent for her to be operated on, as the surgeon was unsure of the cause of her pain. We were told to phone the hospital at 8 pm that night as our daughter would be operated upon at 6 pm, and by 8 pm they would have news for us. Phoning at 8 pm, we were told she was still in the operating theatre and to phone back later. Finally, at 10 pm, we were told that she was out of the operating theatre, but the surgeon wanted to see us at once. As my wife and I drove to the hospital, we both had a sense that this was serious. Had they found cancer? Why had the operation taken so long? Fear and anxiety began rising in our hearts and minds. Then we began to pray in tongues, and suddenly the car was filled with the presence of God. He never promised healing, or anything of that sort to us, but quite simply said, 'It is alright, I'm here.' Never will we forget the wonderful, overwhelming peace that came upon us at that moment. That peace was still with us when the surgeon explained that they had found a cancerous tumour the size of an orange and that it was a very rare form. The peace was still there when a school friend of our daughter, in distress and fear asked us, 'Is she going to die?' She did make a full recovery and is now married with two wonderful children.

What was it that made the difference in both of those situations, on the beach and in the hospital? The awareness of the presence of God. He is faithful who promised, 'Never will I leave you; never will I forsake you. So we say with confidence, "The Lord is my helper; I will not be afraid. What can man do to me?"' (Heb. 13:5–6). In saying he will never leave us, he promises never to withdraw his presence from us. In saying he will not forsake us, he promises never to withdraw his help from us. The availability of his unending presence and help is the reason we can say with confidence, 'I will not be afraid'.

In any period of spiritual attack, we must affirm both

his presence and his help, even when they seem to us to have been withdrawn. Live according to the truth of his word; do not live according to the lie of what seems to be. Remember, Elijah did not die at the hand of Jezebel. God had other ideas for him as well as his end.

The barren time in the life of a prophetic person is only ever a parenthesis and never the final sentence.

Intensity

Another temptation that prophetic people are prone to, as well as being disposed to temperamentally, is that of becoming intense. It is right and understandable that we take our calling and gifting seriously. However, when we are intense most of the time, it is unhealthy and unhelpful. The more intense we become with or in the prophetic, the less effective we become in the end. It is difficult to hear God when one is intense, as we will be more aware of that emotion and attitude than we will be of God's voice. Intensity is often fuelled when we try to be God to people. What I mean by that is, that we put pressure upon ourselves to always have an answer to every question or problem that other people have. We need to realise that if God does not give us an answer, then we do not have one to give. This does not mean we have failed them. Our job should be teaching others how to hear from him for themselves. We must trust the Lord to deal with people and not think it all depends upon us.

NOTES
[1]*Journey Towards Holiness*, Alan Kreider (Marshall Pickering).
[2]KJV (Thomas Nelson, 1976).

Chapter 6

COPING WITH PROPHETIC
PRESSURES AND PAINS

In the last chapter, we looked at some of the pressures
that prophetic people experience and ways to alleviate
them. Here we will look at practical measures we can
take that will enable us to soar and not be earthbound
by the pressures.

The prophetic person may well prefer solitude to
company and, as mentioned before, will require this
solitude at times in order to function effectively: but they
cannot afford to become isolated. They can easily become
self-righteous or self-pitying if left to themselves. In
order to prevent this happening and to keep them
wholesome it is imperative for the prophetic person to:

1. Cultivate good friends

Wisdom is needed here in order that prophetic people do
not find themselves becoming friends with people who,
through their friendship, believe that they will gain easy
access to revelation from God about themselves. Equally,

wisdom is needed so that they do not end up with so-called friends who simply want to use their friendship to either bask in reflected glory or to further their own ministry opportunities. They need friends who they enjoy spending time with. These friends will not only be prophetic people. We all need friends of all different 'shapes and sizes'. Some of my very best friends are not in full-time ministry: one is a rally car driver, another is a businessman, others are excellent Bible teachers, and one is an extremely able theologian. Yes, some are prophetic people too. Variety is, for me, the spice of life here. None of them were chosen by me in order to help with the ministry, but because I liked being with them.

Friends help to keep prophetic people in the 'real world'. They contribute to a well-rounded personality. They are there when times are difficult and when times are easy. They help us to keep a true perspective on things and stop us believing our own publicity. They must be people who are not afraid to tell us the truth about ourselves and, importantly, they do not all have to be at the same level of understanding, maturity, or ability as we are. The more diverse our friends are, the more normal we will be. According to the book of Proverbs, friends are:

- Dependable and loyal – they love at all times (Prov. 17:17). This provides us with security.
- Honest, not flatterers – 'faithful are the wounds of a friend' (Prov. 27:6). This provides us with honest appraisal. It also ensures we have a correct perspective upon things.
- Good counsellors – 'The pleasantness of one's friend springs from his earnest counsel' (Prov. 27:9). This provides us with understanding.

- Sharpeners of our thoughts – 'As iron sharpens iron, so one man sharpens another' (Prov. 27:17). The authorised version adds the word friend in this verse. This provides us with stimulation.

These things are very necessary if we are to wholesomely handle the pressure that being prophetic can bring. The real key to this is in our cultivating and nurturing of friendships. We need to spend time with our friends. We must ensure that we keep in touch with them.

2. Cultivate team relationships

Many unnecessary difficulties are encountered in the lives of prophetic people, simply because they operate from a base of being an isolated individual. They may have friends, but those friends do not form any part of their ministry. Pluralities or teams, are seen everywhere in the New Testament. In the church at Antioch, prophets and teachers met together: this was team. Paul never travelled in ministry alone. He had companions with him who were his team. Even Philip, after preaching to the Samaritans, called for Peter and John to come down from Jerusalem and help: another example of team mentality. Jesus chose his disciples, who accompanied him everywhere and received on-the-job training: this was his team. There is strength in being a team and there is an effectiveness in working as part of a team that is proportionately greater than operating as an individual. The strength that comes from teamwork is referred to in Ecclesiastes 4:12: 'Though one may be overpowered, two can defend themselves. A cord of three strands is not quickly broken.' We are all prone to spiritual attack and it is very comforting to know that we do not have to face attacks by ourselves.

The greater effectiveness of a team compared to an individual is mentioned in Leviticus 26:8: 'Five of you will chase a hundred, and a hundred of you will chase ten thousand, and your enemies will fall by the sword before you'. In other words – we accomplish more together than we can on our own: much more; abundantly more; it is multiplication of result, not just addition.

It is my conviction that prophetic people in a church will be stronger and more effective if they come together as a team or teams (depending upon how many there are or the size of the church). For instance, how effective a prophetic team would be if they met together to pray over issues and as they, together, waited upon God, they could share with one another anything that they felt God was saying to them. Together, they could discuss and weigh this so that when they shared it either publicly, or in private with individuals or the leaders, it would carry the weight of more than one person's private revelation. Of course, these kind of prophetic teams would need to be overseen by someone appointed by the church leaders or by one of the leaders themselves. Another advantage of the prophetic team relationship is that when a prophecy is judged to be defective in some way, then the individual is not left to struggle with this all alone. They can go to the prophetic team for guidance, understanding and insight into the situation. Being part of a prophetic team also means that they are accountable to the team. As mentioned before, prayer and prophecy are very much linked in the Scriptures. It is easy to bring a word and then forget all about it, but some words need to be taken up in intercession. It is here that the prophetic team can make the prophetic person responsible for praying over the word they have brought.

For those who travel, having another prophetic person to travel with is of great benefit, especially if they are part of the prophetic team or a close friend. They relieve the burden of responsibility, as they are there sharing in all that is going on. I have personally found great benefit in having a good friend, Marshall Schiatel, with me on ministry trips. In most of the churches I have visited in the UK, it has been expected that I would do the main preaching and also minister prophetically after the preaching. It has made the task a lot easier to finish speaking and then have Marshall bring any words he has from the Lord, and while he is ministering, I have time to listen to God for anything extra. The relief this brings, means that we can usually hear more and are more than twice as effective.

To be able to truly relax, even when on a ministry trip, is important for the prophetic person's wellbeing. Another good friend and ministry companion, from the USA, Sam Poe, helps me considerably in this area. Sam has a powerful prophetic ministry, and has a sense of humour that is very like my own. He also enjoys looking around shops, which I enjoy too. I remember once being in a restricted access nation with Sam, where the situation was very tense. The meetings had had to be changed because of the possibility of police interference. Every member of the church we were with had been in prison and, as if this were not enough, the leaders wanted us to prophesy over every member in the next meeting. To say the least, anxiety and tension were running very high. Then, the Spirit of God came, and only six hours later did we finish prophesying over the last person, having had only a ten-minute break. It was Sam's company that helped stop fear becoming a problem, and his humour, afterwards, that prevented pride in our success becoming a problem too. Surely, these mutual benefits derived from ministering together are what lay behind Jesus sending the disciples out in pairs.

If you are all on your own, ask for help in becoming part of a team relationship. It can be difficult as we adjust from prophetic isolation to 'prophetic communality', but the blessing and benefits make it very worthwhile. One of the happiest and most effective times of my ministry was when I was part of a team who were all friends. We came to the place, through openly sharing our lives, where we knew that there was nothing hidden from each other. We knew everything there was to know about one another and loved each other just the same. Often, at conferences and events at which the whole team was ministering, people would ask us what was it that we had, which made us so effective and demonstrated so clearly something of the Kingdom of God. The answer was, of course, that we were friends as well as a team.

In becoming a team member, or embarking on a course to become a team member, we ought also, as prophetic people, to:

3. Have a mentor

A mentor is someone who can be an adviser, counsellor, trainer and role model for us. Above all, they must inspire us. They can be part of the same prophetic team but they do not need to be. The all-important criterion is that we have a real relationship with them, not just an acquaintance. Joshua had Moses, the school of the prophets had Samuel, and Elisha had Elijah as their mentors. A mentor is not someone that you admire from a distance, but someone with whom you have a close relationship. This was certainly true of all the above examples. Having a mentor would help prophetic people develop in their gifting and become even more effective.

Soon after my conversion, some forty-five years ago, I met Campbell McAlpine, a prophetic minister of international standing. This gracious man of God took me under his wing and became a spiritual father to me. Initially, I had no understanding of what prophetic ministry was, and I certainly had no aspirations to become one myself. We simply met together and he taught me how to hunger and thirst after God. As the years progressed and my calling became clearer, I viewed him as a mentor in the prophetic. Here was a man who heard from God, was fearless in speaking forth what God showed him, and had one of the largest hearts of love for the body of Christ that I have ever known. I wanted to be like him. He truly inspired me, taught me and motivated me. Now forty-five years later, he is still keeping me on my prophetic toes, often greeting me with, 'what do you believe the Spirit is saying to the church today'. What a friend and mentor.

Never be afraid to approach a person further on in the prophetic than yourself and ask if they would be prepared to help and mentor you. The worst that could happen is that they say no. If that happens, look for another. You will find someone eventually and the benefits will be readily seen. Never feel that you do not need a mentor. This is arrogance at its worst, and not asking is not a sign of humility, but probably of fear or pride. Having a mentor will help you when you are facing pressures, for you will find that there is 'nothing new under the sun' and will discover that your mentor has faced these pressures too. To have a mentor will

ultimately enhance the body of Christ, through its
benefits to you and that is the goal for which you should
aim: not merely your own fulfilment.

In addition to this, prophetic people ought also to have:

4. Specific Prayers

The apostle, Paul, in eight of his epistles (Romans, 2
Corinthians, Ephesians, Philippians, Colossians, 1
Thessalonians, 2 Thessalonians and Philemon) asked the
saints to pray on his behalf. He was very aware that the
effectiveness of his ministry was interconnected with the
prayers that were prayed on his behalf. If that were true of
him, then we too should have people specifically praying
for us. Among the topics he requested prayer for were:

- That his ministry might be acceptable to the saints in
  Jerusalem (Rom.15:31).
- Help in struggles and to have the favour of God
  (2 Cor. 1:11).
- The right words to speak and the boldness to do so
  (Eph. 6:19).
- Help, and deliverance from adversity (Phil. 1:19).
  (This is more recognition of what they had prayed for
  rather than a direct request, but it shows he depended
  on their prayers.)
- For opportunity to speak the message God had given
  him and for clarity in its presentation (Col. 4:3–4).
- General prayers on behalf of himself and his team (1
  Thess. 5:25).
- A rapid spread of the message he proclaimed
  (2 Thess. 3:1).
- Release from prison and restoration to fellowship with
  his friend (Philem. v.22).

Prophetic people will be able to identify with most of the above requests and will find some particularly relevant to them. They should invite specific people to pray for them regularly and these people should be given definite requests. Those requests could include:

- Help in particular pressures we are facing.
- Restoration of confidence to minister.
- That we receive accurate words.

There should be a regular updating of the requests, together with any answers that have been received. The people chosen to pray need not necessarily be those of like gift, or those that are on the same team. Certainly the saints that Paul asked to pray for him were not of the same gifting, nor were they on his team. The important factor is that they are people who will pray.

Whether we are struggling with pressure, pain or wanting to soar again, the prayers of others on our behalf will be very effective in bringing about the desired result. As in all things, we are not left entirely on our own to pray everything through, but we are a part of his glorious body in which there are those who can strengthen us by their prayers.

Chapter 7

SOAR AGAIN

Fortunately for us, the experience of being earthbound, or if you prefer, the experience of finding ones gift has become dormant, is not a new phenomena. It would appear, from Paul's letters to Timothy, that this young man was prone to having the same experience (1 Tim. 4:14 and 2 Tim. 1:6). In the first passage, Timothy is told not to neglect his gift and in the second passage, he is told to fan into flame the gift that is in him. As to what that gift was, commentators are at variance. Gordon Fee, in *God's Empowering Presence* (Hendrickson), says of the gift mentioned in 1 Timothy 4:14, that 'it is probably Timothy's specific giftedness for ministry that is present through the gift of the Spirit' (page 773).[1] Of 2 Timothy 1:6, however, he says the gift was the person of the Spirit himself (page 787). On the other hand, John Rea, in *The Holy Spirit In The Bible* (Marshall Pickering), says that the gift referred to in both passages is that charismatic gift given to all Spirit-baptised believers (pages 305–308).[2] I believe the truth lies in a combination of the two. It is the Holy Spirit within us, who imparts to us one of his gifts. If we neglect being constantly filled with the Spirit, then how can we operate his gifts: but if we neglect (are careless of, make light of) his gifts, allowing them to remain dormant, then we grieve him. The result of both positions is that the gift is not exercised. We then need to 'fan into flame' again the Spirit and his gift. This is made very clear in 2 Timothy 1:6–7: 'For this reason I remind you to fan into flame the gift of God, which is in you through the laying on of my hands. For God did not give us a spirit of timidity, but a spirit of power, of love and of self-discipline'.

Paul's metaphor of fanning into flame suggests that the fire has died down, not that it has gone out. The gift is still there, but it needs to be stirred up; it needs to be operated again. Without doing violence to the text, we could say that it is the same sentiment as saying, 'eagles, fly again, do not remain earthbound'. Your prophetic gift has not been withdrawn, it is only dormant: even if it has been dormant for a very long time. Paul tells Timothy that he must do something about it. It is Timothy's responsibility to fan the embers of his gift into flame once more. While we accept our dormant state, we will never soar again. We have to play an active part in fanning our gift into flame. How can we do this?

It must begin with a desire to fly again. That is, we must have a desire to start operating in our gift again. No methodologies or techniques can possibly replace the need for desire: we must want to. Paul makes this plain in 1 Corinthians 14:1,39. In both verses, he exhorts the Corinthians to be eager in their desire to prophesy. The word translated eager, *zeloo,* means to be zealous in pursuit, to strive after, to exert oneself. It is clearly our responsibility to do something about it: we must not allow ourselves to be, or remain, passive. We could say colloquially, 'fall over yourself' to do it! It is right at this point that we must refuse to allow our desire to become paralysed by entertaining any negative fears that the gifting and ministry we have had in the past will not work again in the present. We must desire, and believe that the God who told us to desire will not leave us frustrated, but rather give us the ability to turn desire into achievement. After all, if he says 'be eager to prophesy', knowing that you will not be able to do so then, far from being a loving Heavenly Father (which is exactly what he is), he would be a frustrating father. He would be like the proverbial farmer who dangles a carrot on a long pole in front of a donkey, knowing that the donkey will never reach the carrot, but, nevertheless, keeping the donkey moving (motivated) towards it. Our Father in Heaven never has been, nor will he be like this towards us.

To desire to prophesy is a specific, positive attitude. It means that we are consciously telling the Lord that we want to begin again, regardless of what it was or is that has kept us back and earthbound. We must not adopt a passive attitude such as, 'well if he wants me to minister it's up to him'. Passivity is the very opposite to the exhortation of Paul to 'be eager to prophesy' (1 Cor. 14:39). It also means that we will go to a meeting being consciously available to the Lord to be used in prophecy at that gathering for the sake of the body, and desiring to be used. If this seems difficult at the moment, why not ask the Holy Spirit to reawaken your desire and quicken it.

There are also times when it is difficult to find the desire, simply because we seem to have run out of energy. The circumstantial pressure in our life may have eroded our motivation, and even the thought of having to desire something saps our emotional and spiritual strength. How then can we begin again?

Elijah knew what it was to be exhausted to the point of despair (1 Kgs. 19:4). He, too, lost his desire to carry on in ministry: "'I have had enough, Lord,' he said. "Take my life'". It is understandable that he was physically exhausted, considering what he had done at, and after, Mount Carmel. He had climbed up and down the mountain twice, then he had run about seventeen miles, to Jezreel. Soon after this, because of Jezebel's threat, he travelled 130 miles to Beersheba and then walked another eighteen or more miles before sitting down and asking to die. Although Elijah was a man of the Spirit, and the power of the Lord came upon him to enable him to run ahead of Ahab to Jezreel, he still had a normal human body, which was subject to limitations as well as to normal physiological responses. After a day such as he had had, he would have been tired and exhausted. Here was the classic fight and flight syndrome leading to exhaustion. Whether we believe that man is a tri-unity of body, soul and spirit, or a bi-unity of body and soul, the fact remains that the constituent parts of man's make-up all interact upon each other. Therefore, we need to take care of each constituent part.

So, what was the answer that would enable Elijah to begin again and leave his despondency behind? Rest, food and drink (1 Kgs. 19:5–8). It should be noted that, at no point in the angel's two visits to Elijah did the angel rebuke him or command him to repent of his current disposition. Elijah was commanded to eat and drink. He needed to rest and to take care of his body's needs in order that he might have fresh energy and thus be able to see the situation in the correct light.

Jesus himself knew the importance of this for the wellbeing of his disciples. When they returned from being sent out in pairs by Jesus to preach, cast out demons and heal the sick, they heard the distressing

news of John the Baptist's death. Jesus' immediate
response to this was, 'Come with me by yourselves to a
quiet place and get some rest' (Mark 6:31).

Many prophetic people find themselves earthbound
and unable even to stir up the desire to fly, simply
because they need a period of recuperation. This is
especially true in the days in which we live. These days
we frequently travel across time lines, leaving us jet-
lagged. We fill our lives with more things to do because
of the convenience of travel etc. We have more meetings
than ever to attend, and conferences abound for us to
participate in. Many have demanding jobs in the so-
called 'secular' world, and wives face the daily demands
of running a home and bringing up children as well.
Eventually, it all catches up with us, and tiredness, if
not sheer exhaustion, can cause us to give up on both
desire and gift.

It is not spiritual to never have time off from ministry.
Workaholics, in the end, do not glorify God. When Moses'
attention was captivated, in the desert, by the burning
bush, it was not due to the fact that the bush was
burning: it was because the bush burned, yet did not
burn up (Exod. 3:2–3). God does not want us to burn out
for him, but to burn on for him. The Sabbath was created
by God, not as a luxury, but as a necessity for living
wholesomely. It was made for the benefit of mankind;
mankind were not made for the benefit of the Sabbath
(Mark 2:27). Unless we make time for rest and
relaxation, we will lose our desire, go stale, and our
gifting will start to become dormant. After a period of
rest, however, the desire to be used again will naturally
return. We should never yield to the belief that God will
keep overriding our bodily needs supernaturally, in
order that we may keep going in ministry. When he does
do that, it is because of exceptional circumstances, for a

limited period. Our bodily needs (especially food, drink, and rest) are, like our emotions, part of God's creation design and cannot continually be ignored without us suffering the consequences.

Music is another means of 'fanning into flame' the prophetic gift. In 2 Kings 3:4–16, the story is told of three kings going to battle. The King of Israel, the King of Judah and the King of Edom joined forces to crush a rebellion by the King of Moab. As these three kings set out to engage the enemy, they found that, after a circuitous march of seven days, they had run out of water for themselves and their animals. The King of Israel wondered if God had brought them together with the purpose of handing them over to the Moabites. The King of Judah asked whether there was a prophet of the Lord that they could seek guidance from. So it was, that the three kings appeared before Elisha wanting a word from the Lord. Elisha, having voiced his disdain for the King of Israel and his respect for the King of Judah, then asked for a harpist to be brought to him. 'While the harpist was playing, the hand of the Lord came upon Elisha' and he prophesied (2 Kings 3:15). The harpist enabled Elisha to prophesy, in what was a difficult situation for him. He was under pressure to bring a word to order, as well as the pressure of having someone before him whom he did not respect at all. Music had a quieting effect upon his spirit, and released the prophetic gifting.

We saw, in Chapter 1 of this book, that David appointed seers to be the musicians in the temple, in order to help release the prophetic. It could have been that David's prophetic psalms were inspired as he played his harp out on the hillside whilst caring for the sheep. Anointed music is a powerful, God-given medium for fanning into flame this gift that God has given us. Earthbound eagles wanting to fly again should soak themselves in praise and worship music. Playing this kind of music in the home, in the car and during devotional times, will both stir up the desire to prophesy and the ability to do so.

As mentioned before, we need to go to meetings having specifically made ourselves available to the Lord to be used to prophesy, but we must not be so focused upon this that we do not enter in to the worship that is going on. Our focus, in worship, should always be upon the Lord, and never simply upon the things of the Lord. If the things of the Lord become our focus, then we are guilty of idolatry. If we ignore the worship because of our intense desire to prophesy, that intensity will work against us. If, on the other hand, we enter in to the worship, we will find that we are being stirred, either to prophesy there and then, or we are receiving from the Lord thoughts that are for communicating at another time or even another place. In either case, we have found that the gift has been fanned into flame by worship.

Returning to 2 Timothy 1:6–7: 'For this reason I remind you to fan into flame the gift of God, which is in you through the laying on of my hands. For God did not give us a spirit of timidity, but a spirit of power, of love and of self-discipline.' Paul suggested to Timothy that the gift had died down through timidity. Literally, the word is 'cowardice'. It can mean to run away from or to want to run away from. The adjective form was used by Jesus when he asked the disciples, 'Why are you so afraid?' on the occasion of the storm on the Sea of Galilee. (Mat. 8:26). They were afraid of the storm they wanted out of the situation. Was timidity Timothy's disposition, or had something happened to cause him to become timid. We are not told, but we do know that he had given into it. It does not matter whether we are timid by nature or have become timid as the result of something. The moment we let our timidity govern us, we will stop using our gift. Timidity is a weakness that inhibits and restrains us. That is why Paul reminds Timothy that God has not given it to us, but he has given to us a spirit of power instead. Jamieson, Fausset and Brown, in their commentary on this verse, point out that 'Power is the invariable accompaniment of the gift of the Holy Ghost'.[3] Acts 1:8, links 'power' and 'the Spirit' together: 'But you will receive power when the Holy Spirit comes on you'. This power will override our natural tendencies. *Strong's Concordance* says of this word power: 'inherent power, power residing in a thing by virtue of its nature, or which a person or thing exerts and puts forth'.[4] When we receive the Holy Spirit, we receive his inherent power and thus we can exercise that power to overcome our weaknesses. Again, Jamieson, Fausset and Brown helpfully point out that, 'Fear within exaggerates the causes of fear without. The "spirit of power" is the spirit of man, dwelt in by the Spirit of God imparting power.'[5] To enable us to stir up the gift that we have, and to overcome our timidity, we need to reaffirm and to believe that:

a) Our timidity is not of God
   and
b) that the Holy Spirit is sufficient for overcoming our reticence and for us to begin again.

However, Paul not only speaks of power in this verse, but of love and self-discipline as reasons for and ways of stirring up the gift. Love for God and mankind is the only true motivation for desiring and operating spiritual gifts (1 Cor. 13). Neither threats, nor inducements will enable us to stir up the prophetic gift, but love will. Love will also restore the desire to move again in the prophetic. Put simply, if we love God, we will want to be available to be used by him, as he desires. If we love others, we will want to bless them by revealing to them something of God's heart, mind, will and purpose. The problem is: how can I love God and others like this, and thereby stir up the gift?

The answer lies, again, in the Holy Spirit. On one occasion, in Southampton, I heard Mike Bickle, of Metro Christian Fellowship, Kansas City, America, say that it takes God to love God. So, if I am to love God, I need God to do the loving through me. That is exactly what the Holy Spirit does for us. In Romans 5:5, Paul states: 'God has poured out his love into our hearts by the Holy Spirit, whom he has given us.' The tense used here means that God has poured, and continues to pour (abundantly and copiously), out his love into our hearts. This is not just a one-time experience but an ongoing experience. To rekindle both the desire to stir up the gift and to stir up the gift itself, I need the Holy Spirit to keep filling me with the love of God. I also need to recognise that God has given this to me and wants to give even more of this to me. Therefore, I need to ask him continually, to fill me with his love and to keep me in his love.

There is a temptation for prophetic people to query God's love for them when they have experienced being earthbound for some time. No matter what the reason for this experience, the enemy of our souls will use the experience to cast doubt upon God's unconditional love for us. We invariably turn inwards upon ourselves and, as we can never find anything we have done that merits God's love, we wrongly conclude that he cannot love us or that his love for us has diminished, and we give up believing that we can begin to prophesy again. We lose heart. The answer never lies in our looking into ourselves: it lies in looking unto Jesus.

The writer of the book of Hebrews emphatically states that, by fixing our eyes upon Jesus and considering his suffering, we will not grow weary and lose heart (Heb. 12:2–5). To fix our eyes upon Jesus simply means that we give him our attention: expecting to receive something from him. This is what the lame man did to Peter and John as they went past him at the temple gate called Beautiful. In response to the crippled beggar's request for money, Peter commanded him, 'Look at us'. The beggar 'gave them his attention, expecting to get something from them' (Acts 3: 1–5). This was an act of faith. We have to believe that, as we pay attention to Jesus, ie obey his word, grace to help us will be forthcoming.

In order to know that, in spite of our circumstances or performance, God loves us, we need to look at the suffering of Jesus. We are given an insight into his suffering, as Jesus approached the end of his earthly life, in the Garden of Gethsemane. In their accounts of Jesus in Gethsemane, Matthew, Mark and Luke all use different words in the Greek to bring out the intensity of Jesus' agony. Matthew, in chapter 26:37–38, uses three different words which, translated, mean *sorrowful, troubled,* and *overwhelmed. Sorrowful:* to be in heaviness, grief, to make one uneasy. *Troubled:* great distress. It is the strongest word in the New Testament for depression. *Overwhelmed:* overcome so much with sorrow as to cause death. Mark writes (Mark 14:33–34) of Jesus being deeply *distressed:* a word that, in Greek, means to be thrown into terror, to be thoroughly alarmed. Finally Luke, in chapter 22:44 uses the word *anguish,* which meant severe mental struggles and emotions: like the struggle of two Olympic wrestlers fighting for supremacy.

What was it that reduced Jesus to such a mental and emotional state? Why did he experience such depth of terror? There can only be one answer: because he was looking into the face of divine wrath. The wrath of God against sin is so terrible that 'the kings of the earth, the princes, the generals, the rich, the mighty, and every slave and every free man hid in caves and among the rocks of the mountains. They called to the mountains and the rocks, "Fall on us and hide us from the face of him who sits on the throne and from the wrath of the lamb! For the great day of their wrath has come, and who can stand?"' (Rev. 6: 15–17). He faced and endured this in order that we might look into the face of divine acceptance. In the midst of Gethsemane and Calvary, he found the strength to endure both, because he contemplated the joy of spending eternity with us. That was the joy that was set before him and that is the extent of his magnificent love for us.

To soar again, we need to constantly affirm that God loves us totally, and the grounds for that is not my circumstances or my feelings and never my performance as a Christian, but the suffering and death of his wonderful son on my behalf. 'But God demonstrates his own love for us in this: While we were still sinners, Christ died for us' (Rom. 5:8). Our view of the suffering of Christ should not focus so much on what we did to him, as it should upon what he has done for us.

Paul also spoke to Timothy of the need for self-discipline. This meant that Timothy must not entangle himself with affairs that were not relevant to his calling. The issue was not whether the things Timothy had become entangled with were of themselves right or wrong, but were they appropriate and of priority to him: whether those things were helpful or unhelpful to a soldier of Jesus Christ. If we are to stir up the prophetic gift, then we must not allow ourselves to be diverted from our calling to move in the prophetic. Neither must we indulge in things, although harmless of themselves, which rob us of the time and opportunity to meet with God: out of which our gifting will flow. We have to live disciplined lives in the areas of personal devotions, study, and seeking God. However, it is not only in the matter of time that we must be self-disciplined, but also with what we fill our time.

It is important that we listen to God during the time we set apart for him, as well as at other times. Listening to God must be part of the content of our disciplined time. Listening to God is a necessity if we are to have any confidence that we have a word to give. 1 Corinthians 14:30–31 says: 'And if a revelation comes to someone who is sitting down, the first speaker should stop. For you can all prophesy in turn.' In Bible times, teachers sat to deliver their message, but prophets stood to deliver theirs. When Jesus taught his disciples in the Sermon on the Mount (Matt. 5:1–2) it says: 'He sat down. His disciples came to him and he began to teach them.' Likewise, when he taught the crowd by the lake of Gennesaret (Luke 5:1–3), he got into a boat and sat down and taught. When he prophesied in the temple about the coming of the Spirit it says 'Jesus stood and said in a loud voice' (John 7:37). Therefore, in the Corinthian passage, the person who wanted to exercise the gift of prophecy would have stood in the assembly to indicate this so that others could make room for the contribution. If the person was to make such a public indication that they had a prophetic word to give, then they must have been reasonably confident. See David's assurance in the fulfilling of God's word to him through the resurrection of Jesus (Acts 2:30–31) and Elijah's confidence in his prophetic word that it would not rain unless he said so (1 Kgs. 17:1). How could all these people be so confident? Because they listened.

Listening also allows us to know something of God's purposes. Jeremiah tells of the false prophets who were operating in his day (Jer. 23). In verses 18 and 22 he says that part of their problem was that they did not stand in the council of the Lord in order to see or hear his word and neither did they listen to him. The word council, here, has two meanings. The first is a secret or confidential talk. The second is a group of intimates with whom one shares confidential matter. The picture here is of a person or people sitting listening to God who, in return, is sharing revelation with them. In the Jeremiah context, this would have been about his purposes for Israel ie their going into captivity. Listening to God takes patience and persistence: for sometimes, the word from God takes a long time to come and, therefore, we can become discouraged.

In listening to God, we need to ensure that we resist any temptation to regard ourselves as special, simply because we have a prophetic calling. We are no more special than anybody else in the Body of Christ. If we allow ourselves to begin thinking that we are special, then we open a door for pride and arrogance, which will quickly overcome us and hinder our calling.

Many prophets in the Old Testament went through experiences that dealt a deathblow to their pride. Moses suffered rejection by the Israelites, which caused him to flee from Egypt. He then spent forty years being a shepherd instead of a prince. Isaiah had a remarkable vision of the glory of God in the temple, which caused him to cry out, 'Woe to me! . . . I am ruined!' (Isa. 6:5). Jeremiah, on the other hand, experienced life-long rejection of his message. We must understand that our prophetic ability is a grace-given calling and enabling, and nothing whatsoever to do with being special. Even if others see the prophet as special, we must resist giving in to this temptation.

To safeguard our listening, we also need to be devourers of God's word. This will help to keep us from receiving and giving words that are unbiblical in their content. The content of any prophetic word must never contravene God's written word, the Bible. We need, as well, to be unhurried in our listening. Pray until the presence of God fills you and brings rest to your spirit. Always beware of voices that rush in upon you, as well as anything that creates within you an inordinate sense of hurry. Our listening to God will be safeguarded if we walk in repentance and obedience. We need to be as instantly repentant and obedient as it is possible to be, and not delay either of them.

In Chapter 3, we saw that one cause of becoming earthbound was stress. The very nature of our calling means that we will suffer stress, but we must learn to keep it within acceptable limits, otherwise we and our ministry will suffer unduly. In order to limit stress and its effects in our lives, it is helpful to understand what type of prophetic person is most likely to suffer undue stress and to understand the type of person who is most likely to keep stress under control. Once we know the traits of those who are most prone to stress, and the traits of those who can best handle stress; identifying those traits in our own lives will enable us to take steps to remedy them. In the remedy lies our ability to soar again.

Prophetic people most likely to suffer undue stress

1. Those who are gratified mainly by accomplishment

They will see life and ministry only in terms of results. They will rarely be satisfied with themselves and, therefore, will rarely be satisfied by others. Of course, some will be very accepting of others, whilst being extremely hard upon themselves. They will often feel that others achieve, but not them. Striving and driving soon become the characteristics of their lives and, inevitably, stress results. The Scriptures constantly bear witness to the fact that our gratification should come from our relationship with the Lord, and not only from what we accomplish.

2. Those who find it difficult to get on with others

For these people, the work, or cause, is always more important than people. They forget that the work *is* people; the church *is* people. In the name of being prophetic, these people will sacrifice relationships to quote 'seek the Lord', when the reality is that they don't like being with people. God created us as relational beings: 'It is not good for man to be alone' (Gen. 2:18). We need to be around people in order to retain a true perspective on life, especially when we are going through times of struggle or difficulty. During such times, the temptation is to withdraw from people, but this will only add to the problem, not relieve it.

Being in the presence of others, and enjoying them, helps to prevent us from becoming unreal and also becomes a healthy way of unwinding. When we withdraw from people habitually, it will not be long before unacceptable stress levels start rising in us.

3. Those who are afraid to be themselves

Such people put unrealistic expectations upon themselves, as well as trying most of the time to live up to the expectations of others. The disciples of Jesus were so secure with him, that they were never afraid to let their true humanity show. To constantly be portraying an image other than what you really, are will cause the symptoms of stress to start appearing in your life.

4. Those who are more busy with the work of God, than with God himself

Whatever our calling to the Body of Christ is, God has never principally looked for a workforce, but for a family, indeed a bride, for his son. As the puritans said: 'Man's chief end is to glorify God and to enjoy him forever.' He is not simply our boss, but our Father, and we must learn to enjoy him for himself and not only to have time for his work. All work and no play, not only makes Jack a dull boy, but soon makes all of us stressed-out people. The title of an article I once read on the devotional life put it this way: 'Busyness in the King's business is no excuse for neglecting the King'. It is only as we regularly fellowship with the Lord, that we can make sure that we do not replace him as the focal point of our living, with his work. When the work of God becomes more important to us than God himself, we are definitely headed for undue stress in our lives.

In order to soar again, we must start to deal with any of these attitudes that we find resident in our lives. We must adjust our thinking about these matters and, if necessary, ask for help in overcoming them.

Prophetic people most likely to endure stress

1. Those who know their identity and worth

This knowledge frees them from the need to impress others, for they know that their worth is based, not on achievement, but upon Christ's assessment. It is our position in him, not our performance for him, which gives us identity and value. We had the highest value placed by God upon us before we were even born for, in order that he might have us as his children, he paid the highest price ever in the whole universe: the death of his son. 'For you know that it was not with perishable things such as silver or gold that you were redeemed . . . but with the precious blood of Christ' (1 Pet.1:18–19).

2. Those with a clear understanding of the Body of Christ

We are members one of another. The teaching on the Body of Christ found in 1 Cor. 12–14, emphasises our need of each other. We are not carrying the work of the Lord on our shoulders alone. It is not all up to us as an individual, but it is up to us as a corporate body, within which each individual plays their part. When we truly understand the Body of Christ, we will then see that it is more important to love one another, than it is simply to get the job done at any price. The great commission to preach the gospel to the whole world followed the great commandment to love God and one another. It is not a question of either/or, but of priority.

3. Those with a strong relationship with God

This is not meant to imply that those who suffer from undue stress do not have a strong relationship with God, for sometimes it is only their relationship with God that enables them to keep going. However, it is true that those with a strong relationship with the Lord are less likely to suffer from undue stress. Isaiah says: 'those who hope in the Lord will renew their strength. They will soar on wings like eagles; they will run and not grow weary, they will walk and not be faint' (Isa. 40:31).

David's relationship with God when he was a shepherd, as well as when he was King, could only be described as one of intimacy and strength. It was a relationship that had been developed over the years, so that when he faced times of stress such as the death of his child by Bathsheba, and the rebellion of his son Absalom, his trust in God remained unshakeable. He was able to endure both, as well as many other stress-inducing circumstances, without collapsing under their weight. Prophetic people must, as an absolute priority, maintain guard and develop their personal walk with God.

NOTES

[1]*God's Empowering Presence,* Gordon Fee (Hendrickson Publishers, 1994). Used with permission.

[2]*The Holy Spirit in the Bible,* John Rea (Marshall Pickering, 1992).

[3]*Bethany Parallel Commentary on the New Testament,* Jamieson, Faussett & Brown (©1983 Bethany House Publishers). Used with permission.

[4]*Strong's Exhaustive Concordance,* James Strong (Thomas Nelson, 1996). Used with permission.

[5]*Bethany Parallel Commentary on the New Testament,* Jamieson, Faussett & Brown (©1983 Bethany House Publishers). Used with permission.

Chapter 8

GROWING AS AN EAGLE

As prophetic people, we can never reach a point where we no longer need to develop or grow in our gifting. It is the same for the person who has been exercising their ministry for a considerable length of time as it is for the person just beginning, or for the person starting again.

This chapter will concentrate on some of the ways in which we can grow in the prophetic. Some will be well known, but may have been overlooked in your life with the passage of time. Others may be quite new, in which case, give them serious consideration. Those for whom there is nothing new, or anything they need to be reminded of, please find a prophetic person who is further along in the ministry than yourself and ask them to help you to go further still. Here are some of the more important ways that I have discovered which will help us grow in the prophetic.

Speaking in tongues

This may seem surprising, as Paul writes of speaking in tongues and prophesying as being two distinct gifts.

However, here we are not dealing with the gift of tongues, as used in the gathering of the church, but praying in tongues in private. When Christians speak in tongues, they are expressing their innermost thoughts and feelings in a language that God hears and understands. Praying in tongues is not merely a way of praying when we are not sure of what or how to pray. It expresses to God the deep desires of our hearts, together with the deep feelings that prophetic people have. This expressing of ourselves in prayer opens the way for God's answer, which will result in growth of ourselves and our gift. John Rea, in his book *The Holy Spirit In The Bible* (page 267), asserts that, 'Many are discovering that praying in tongues opens the door for the Holy Spirit to deal with our spirits in the area of subconscious attitudes and desires. So here is an aid in bringing every thought of our minds captive to the obedience of Christ' (2 Cor.10:5).[1]

This means that tongues, besides their other benefits, are a great help in fine-tuning our spirit to God's. It makes listening to God and hearing him so much clearer. A very dear friend of mine, who has a prophetic ministry of outstanding accuracy in the realm of words of knowledge, confided in me that he, regularly, spent a long time each day and before a meeting speaking in tongues. He believed this aided him in receiving words from God in the meeting that followed.

Praying in tongues is a means of building oneself up and, therefore, should be regularly practised by all Christians, and especially prophetic people. They definitely need to be strengthened constantly and they need to retain the cutting edge in their ministry, if they are to grow in the prophetic. We never outgrow the need to pray in tongues regularly. Tongues do not have a limited time value in the life of the believer. Paul was speaking in tongues more than all the Corinthian believers, twenty years after his conversion.

Do not despise or devalue this gift as a means of growing in the prophetic.

Read

The Apostle Paul was evidently a keen reader, who found it a necessity to have reading material to hand. He asks Timothy, in 2 Timothy 4:13, to bring to him his cloak, the books, and especially the parchments. Exactly what these books and parchments were, we cannot be certain, but it is clear that Paul needed written material to be available to him.

I am constantly surprised by two extreme positions that some prophetic people adopt. One is, that they never read anything relating to the prophetic, other than the Bible. The other is, that they devour every book on prophecy they can lay their hands on, yet rarely move in it or grow in it themselves. The former type, tends toward superiority in attitude, and often does not progress very far prophetically beyond the point they have already reached. Possibly the worst expression of this position, is a prophetic utterance that is comprised of Bible verses strung together and delivered in the language of the Authorised Version. These people appear to be afraid of copying something they have read, or else they exhibit unhealthy traits of pride and independence. The latter type, become intellectual experts on prophecy, but have very limited personal experience. To avoid both extremes, we should read extensively, books on the prophetic and books on prophets, together with the Scriptures. We should then seek to put into practice in our lives and ministry that which we have learnt. My life and ministry have been greatly enriched by reading books by authors who have a different slant than me, or who are of a different persuasion than me. We grow by opening ourselves to the writings of people who have insights that we may never have heard of, or seen before. We must never think that only people of our own persuasion (ie denomination, network, or theological interpretation) have all the truth regarding a subject. If we do, we will miss large areas of enlightenment and understanding that would have helped us to develop in our ministry. Far too many people are afraid of even reading works by Christians of differing views, in case they are led into error. It is time that they stopped being afraid of imbibing erroneous teaching and started trusting the Holy Spirit to guide them into truth: which is what he does. Clive Garrett, writing in *Proclaim: Issue no. 9* (Springwood Trust), says of a prophet's reading habits:

> The purpose of reading is not to amass a certain level of information, but to enter into a dialogue with God about what he is reading. The prophet must have the freedom to find stimulation in whatever comes to hand, if God begins to open up concepts from a particular piece of writing. He must not be afraid of what is so often labelled 'unsound' by others, but he must equally be prepared to lay aside any piece of literature in which he discerns a bad spirit. Our protection from error is to walk closely with God.[2]

That great twentieth century prophet, A. W. Tozer, was indebted to the writings of the Christian mystics. He did not endorse all their theology or practices, but what he valued was their utter devotion to God and their ability to share their spiritual insights. Tozer often remarked, 'You can be straight as a gun barrel theologically, and as empty as one spiritually' (*In Pursuit Of God,* pages 155–159, James L. Snyder).[3] Perhaps that was why his emphasis was not on systematic theology, but on a personal relationship with God. The issue in the end will always be, not how much you know, but how well do you know God.

Scripture

Prophetic people need to study, and to meditate on, the Scriptures. The book of Revelation, the great prophetic book of the New Testament, quotes or alludes to the Old Testament 245 times. Its author, John, who claims to be a prophet (Rev. 10:11; 22:9), is definitely steeped in the Old Testament Scriptures, especially those of Isaiah, Jeremiah, Daniel, Ezekiel and Zechariah.

Prophecy is not always a spontaneous thought, in terms of content. The content of a prophetic word may well be the result of our study and meditation of the Scripture. Sometimes, the cause of a continuing low level of content in prophetic utterances is the low priority given to study and meditation. We must remember that the spontaneous element of a prophetic word is often related more to the timing of it, than the content of it.

Another reason for prophetic people to study and meditate on the Scriptures is, in order for them to become acquainted with God's symbolic language. This will help them in the interpreting of dreams, visions and certain prophetic utterances that use figurative language. Although the interpreting of prophetic dreams and visions is an ability given to us by the Holy Spirit, it is, nevertheless, helpful to have an understanding of the way God uses symbols and figurative speech in Scripture. One only has to read the book of Revelation to see that prophetic language is often symbolic. Throughout Scripture, God uses symbols: for instance, water and fire are symbols of the Holy Spirit, but are also used to speak of judgement. The symbol of a sword can represent either, the word that penetrates, or judgement.

Then there is figurative language. Consider how long it has been since Jesus returned to heaven and promised that he would come again soon (Rev. 22:7,12,20). God's understanding of soon and our understanding of the same word are clearly of a different order. Take the Greek word, *Hora,* translated hour. This is used in the Bible to mean: a literal hour, a day, an instant, short, or a season (c/f John 11:9; Mat. 10:19).

The more we absorb the Scripture into our lives, the greater the reservoir we have for the Holy Spirit to highlight and apply when stirring us to prophesy. It is cause for shame and embarrassment, when prophetic people are clearly superficial in their knowledge and approach to Scripture. Prophecy never supersedes or replaces the need for the written word of God. Paul is emphatic on this at the end of 1 Corinthians 14, when he states that his apostolic writing has the Lord's authority: 'If anybody thinks he is a prophet or spiritually gifted, let him acknowledge that what I am writing to you is the Lord's command. If he ignores this, he himself will be ignored' (v.37–38). That kind of apostolic authority lies only in the written Scriptures, and not with a person, however gifted they are.

Spiritual equipment

In Scripture, prophets experienced other gifts accompanying their prophetic ministry. They moved in words of knowledge, miracles, signs, as well as experiencing visions and angelic visitations.

There is no need for the prophetic person to be afraid of asking God to further equip them in their ministry and to make the ministry increasingly effective by the use of these and other gifts and experiences. Jesus taught us to ask the Father, unashamedly, for good gifts (Matt. 7:11). In the context of the passage, earthly fathers are giving to their children those things that are necessary to support their lives. How much more, then, will our Heavenly Father give us good gifts to support our spiritual lives and our ministry. We are not seeking gifts for the sake of experiences, but we are seeking God for gifts to further equip us in our ministry. It is good, therefore, to be specific in our requests and not to generalise in our asking. Having asked, we then need to explore gifts and experiences that subsequently come, or happen to us, and not be afraid of them. Do not write such things off too early as being, 'just me', 'my imagination' etc. It is as we follow through on them that we both develop in our gifting and learn discernment.

I remember vividly, my first angelic visitation, which was accompanied by an unfolding vision of a city. I was so scared, I literally ran away from it before the words that were being spoken were finished. I have often wondered what I would have heard, had I stayed to listen. My second angelic visitation happened when I was in a foreign country. I awoke one morning in that dreamy state between being asleep and fully awake. I was conscious of a light in the bedroom, but this time, instead of being scared, I lay expectantly, eager to experience something of God. Sure enough, I saw two angels, one on each side of the bed, who leant over and touched my chest, and then disappeared. Now nobody knew that, prior to my leaving for this country, and during my first two days there, I had been suffering from severe pains in my chest. They had caused me to become very anxious. However, as I got up and went about the day's business, I found that I no longer had any pains or anxiety. Later that night, whilst I was in a meeting, a prophetess came to me and said: 'Two angels came to you this morning' and then proceeded to tell me why and what they were sent for. As she finished her prophecy, she said, 'and by the way, there is nothing wrong with your heart'. At that time, I had not told anyone at all about the visitation or the pains. In the first instance of angelic visitation, I never followed through on it, but in the second I did, believing that the Lord was giving to me, in love, something which, at that time, was very unusual in my experience.

On another occasion, I was praying in my office when, in my mind's eye, I saw a meeting in progress involving a friend of mine in a country across the other side of the world. My friend was being criticised by others in the meeting, and some were saying hurtful things to her. As I watched this being played in my imagination, God gave me a word about comfort and the ending of difficult times for her. I phoned my friend and was told by her secretary that she was just coming out of a meeting and asked if I would wait. When my friend came to the phone, she told me how she had just left a meeting with her workers, how they had said hurtful things to her and how down she felt. She described exactly what I had seen in my mind. I told her that I had been in the meeting, as it were, and that God had given me a word. When I told her what it was, she wept and said it was so applicable and comforting. I could have written it off as being the product of an over-active imagination, but I have learnt to follow through on the unusual happenings in my life and ministry.

We must not be so afraid of making mistakes that we never move beyond the confines of our normal experiences. As I mentioned earlier, there is a proverb, which says: 'The man who never made a mistake, never made anything.' This is how we grow.

Prophets and prophecies

According to Ephesians chapter 4, the ministry gifts are given for the equipping of the saints. A major help in the growth of prophetic people are established prophets or established prophetic ministries. I am not talking here of having a mentor (I dealt with that in a previous chapter), but of talking to other prophets whenever we have the opportunity. These men and women are a storehouse of experience and knowledge, and time spent with them is an investment for our lives and ministry. I meet regularly throughout the year with prophets, both men and women, from other networks and denominations. As we talk together and share experiences, the benefit I derive is incalculable. There are times of stretching one's thinking and times of confirmation, as we discover that we are all hearing or thinking similar things. Several people from different churches have approached me and asked if they could simply come and spend time talking with me about the prophetic. I am always glad to be available to them, as time allows, and I know that others are also happy to be available to those who want to grow in their gifting.

Another way of growing is, by paying attention to other prophecies and looking for similarities in them to that which you have been hearing from God. From time to time, a prophecy or prophecies are heard that have a far wider significance than just the original hearers. When we become aware of such a prophetic word, we need to link in with it, by paying attention to it and asking God if he wants to show us anything more. Paul's usage of the words 'in part' and 'poor reflection' relating to prophecy, in 1 Corinthians 12:9 and 13, suggest incompleteness. Such prophetic words may not tell the whole story, and may need other prophetic words to complete the picture. At the end of each prophecy to the seven churches, in chapters 2 and 3 of Revelation, there is a phrase used that is common to each of the seven prophecies: 'He who has an ear, let him hear what the Spirit says to the churches'. Now each church is given a specific and distinct message, yet the author does exhort them to hear not only what the Spirit says to the church, singular, but what the Spirit says to the churches, plural. That means there is something in each message that is to be heeded by all.

On one occasion, I had prophesied to a local meeting of leaders about a time coming, when workers from our network would be buried abroad. Sometime (many months) later, at a wider gathering of leaders from our network, Jim Paul, from Canada, who was just passing through, prophesied to the gathering about martyrs that would come from our ranks. The two prophecies needed to be viewed together. The 'local' word needed to be linked into the 'wider' word, for the fullest impact of both. It was this that led me to realise that I must listen carefully to what God is saying to others, and I will grow in understanding and revelation as a result.

Then, of course, there are conferences. Some are specifically about the prophetic, and others have prophetic ministry as a part of the conference. By prioritising conferences, and being selective, so that one does not spend all their time in conferences alone, they can be a valuable means of development. Details of such conferences can be found in most Christian magazines and also from: Graham Cooke, PO Box 91, Southampton, SO15 5ZE, United Kingdom.

NOTES

[1] *The Holy Spirit In The Bible,* John Rea (Marshall Pickering)

[2] *Proclaim: Issue no. 9,* Clive Garret (Springwood Trust). Used with permission.

[3] *In Pursuit Of God,* James L. Snyder quoting A. W. Tozer (©Christian Publications, 1991). Used with permission.

Chapter 9

REPRODUCING EAGLES

It is a law of creation that like begets like. Humans beget humans, not birds or fishes and vice versa. So it is in the spiritual realm: evangelists should produce, through discipling, other evangelists. The same is true for all the ministries and, therefore, prophetic people should reproduce other prophetic people.

In Chapter 6, we spoke of the need to have a mentor to help us. In this chapter, we will deal with the need for us to be a mentor. In the past, too many prophetic people have been left to get on with it by themselves. They have had to face the struggles that accompany prophetic ministry, as well as developing that ministry without anyone being on hand to help them. This is both unhelpful and unbiblical. Maturity and effectiveness in prophetic ministry is not innate, but rather, it is learnt. Our calling to any ministry is a sovereign act of God, and cannot be earned or produced. We learn our skills and ability in the expression of our ministry.

When Jesus called his disciples, he said, 'Come, follow me . . . and I will make you fishers of men' (Mark 1:17).

The disciples became fishers of men as a result of Jesus' training. They were not, although fishermen by trade, automatically equipped to be 'fishers of men'. The call was immediately effective, but they had to be made into the product of the call. The same is true for prophetic people. God calls them to be prophetic, but then they have to be 'made' into effective prophetic ministers. This making is achieved, amongst other things, by we who are already established in the prophetic ministry discipling those who have a similar calling. By the word discipling I mean helping, training, mentoring another.

How do we begin this and what do we do? The first principle for us to adopt is this: we must take the initiative in choosing the person to disciple. This principle appears throughout the Scriptures: Moses chose Joshua, Elijah chose Elisha, Jesus chose the twelve disciples, and Paul chose Timothy. Even if someone approaches us first, we are the one who makes the final decision as to whether or not we will disciple them. Choosing someone to disciple must not be a hasty decision. The decision must be based upon prayer, potential, and proof.

Prayer

Before Jesus made the selection of the twelve apostles from amongst his disciples, he had spent the whole of the previous night in prayer (Luke 6:12–13). Praying before such an important decision will help to keep us free from either personal prejudice or personal preference. We need to ask the Lord if he has any objection to the names we are bringing before him. In prayer, we can also receive prophetic revelation regarding whom we should choose. If we believe that the Lord guides us continually (Isa.

58:11), and that he instructs and teaches us in the way we should go (Ps. 32:8), then we can trust him to make his will very clear to us in this matter.

I always approach the will of God from a positive base. That is why I would assume, in the matter of choosing disciples, that my choice was right, unless God showed me to the contrary, rather than assuming my choice to be suspect unless he gave me clear, specific affirmation. If, at any stage of praying about who you are to disciple, you feel disquiet or unease about a person, then do not proceed any further with that choice. The unease may have nothing to do with their morality or spirituality and must not be interpreted as such. It may be that you are simply not the right person to disciple them. Unless God clearly reveals the reason to you, make no assumptions whatsoever.

The people I will bring before God in prayer will be those that have initially come to mind, as a result of observing in them potential for prophetic ministry.

Potential

Potential in a person is an indicator, not a guarantee. If there are no signs of potential for a prophetic ministry, then it is unlikely that the person in question can develop one. Where there is potential, then discipling is the means of turning potential into achievement. It is therefore of great importance that we know what to look for in a person, which indicates prophetic potential. There are many things, and the following list is by no means exhaustive or definitive, but some, at least, of those mentioned should be observable in a person's life.

1. A tendency to be visionary

This does not mean that they are having visions, but that they are looking further ahead than most: they can see the bigger picture of the purposes of God. They will be people who are certain of what should be built, but uncertain or even at a loss to know how it should be built.

2. Use of the gift of prophecy

Prophetic words should be brought by them, fairly regularly.

3. Having a passionate burden

This is one of the hallmarks of the prophets in Scripture. No cold, analytical rationalism motivated them, or formed the content of their message. They were passionate in their proclaiming and content, for they were conscious of representing the heart of God. His fire burned in them.

4. Serious about developing in the prophetic

There should be a willingness to be inconvenienced for the sake of developing the ministry. I knew a person who was always telling me that they wanted to spend time with me in order to develop their prophetic ministry, but they never made any arrangements to meet with me. In the end, I realised that they wanted me to chase them, instead of them pursuing me. Needless to say, nothing has ever developed.

5. *Excited and motivated by prophetic ministry*

All types of ministry should stir, challenge and inspire us but, for the prophetic person, it will be the prophetic ministry that really fires their imagination. They will find this to be so, even before they realise that they are prophetic.

6. *A person of prayer and a lover of times alone with God*

The first mention of a prophet in the Bible is Abraham, in Genesis 20:7. Here, the ministry of the prophet is linked to prayer. Abraham, at this point, has not prophesied, but nevertheless, God calls him a prophet and says that because of this, he will pray for Abimelech. Prayer flows out from Abraham's calling not the other way around.

When looking for prayer as a sign of prophetic potential, we must not confuse being a person of prayer with the length that one prays. Instead, we need to look for a love of praying and regularity in praying. It is better that a person prays for five minutes every day and looks forward to it, than they pray occasionally for thirty minutes and find it a chore.

In the New Testament, before Jesus commenced his ministry, John the Baptist was the outstanding prophet of his day. We are told very little about John's life between his being born and his appearing on the scene as a preacher of repentance. What we are told is that he lived in the desert until he appeared publicly, and that it was while he was in the desert that the word of the Lord came to him (Luke 1:80; 3:2). He was obviously alone with God during this time. For the prophetic person, enjoying time alone with God is paramount. Again, we are not concerned about the length of this time, but the attitude that is manifested towards such times.

Unrealised potential is the cause of many regrets and much sadness in a person's life. This is also true of a discipler when they see the disciple's potential unrealised. As mentioned previously, potential is an indication, not a guarantee. However, there is something the discipler should take into account, other than potential, when choosing someone to disciple. That is, the person's proven track record or history.

Proof

We are not talking here, primarily, of proven ability in the prophetic, or in any other form of public ministry. We are looking for a history (no matter how short) of loyalty, integrity, servanthood and commitment. Disciples in the prophetic need to show proof of character, not simply potential of charisma.

We are not looking for perfection in their character, but we are looking for basic desires for godliness and righteous living. John and Paula Sandford present this powerfully in their book, *The Elijah Task,* saying:

An older prophet trained a younger prophet by humiliating him, crushing and breaking his pride, defeating him and revealing his smallness and incapability before God. Test after test was put upon the neophyte. The test was a success, only if he *failed* to pass it! To learn that he could not succeed by his own soul's resources was the first building block and constant checkpoint of the prophet's study course. Whatever showed the prophet his inner rotten core and brought him to despair of conquering it, was a success, for it had taken away another 'reason for confidence in the flesh' (Phil.3:4).[1]

Even Isaiah was not perfect when God called him to be a prophet. He confesses this in Isaiah 6:5, as he cries, 'I am ruined! For I am a man of unclean lips'.

Probably the greatest qualification for ministry is the realisation of our utter inadequacy to fulfil it. However, we must not stop at this, for we must see that, though we are inadequate, when God calls, he also equips. Moses was certainly aware of his shortcomings, but what made God rebuke him was Moses' refusal to believe that God had resources in himself, sufficient for Moses to be and to do what God had planned (Exod. 4:10–17).

Having made our choice of who we want to disciple in the prophetic, we then have to do it.

The training

This training, or discipling, of a prophetic person will take place as they are, simply, with the one doing the discipling. When Jesus chose his twelve disciples, it was in order that 'they might be with him and that he might send them out to preach and to have authority to drive out demons' (Mark 3:14–15). The sending out of his disciples came from their being with him: observing his life and his ministry was, for them, a learning process. Their request to be taught to pray followed hard upon their observation of Jesus' prayer life (Luke 11:1–2).

Adequately discipling someone requires spending time with them. There will be times of formal instruction, informal instruction, and observation of the discipler's life and ministry. The one being discipled will also serve the discipler: not in a servile way, or fulfilling the other's every whim, but in order to learn from and assist the other's ministry. Graham Perrins says 'The foundation of all prophetic ministry is to live in the realm of the mundane and menial and yet see the shadow of God's glory over it all' *(Prophetic Bulletin)*.[2] Even Elisha was known as the one who poured water on Elijah's hands (2 Kgs. 3:11). This was the act of a servant. The word is used in this context of important service of a personal nature.

The person doing the discipling should set tasks for the disciple. These ought to be theoretical and practical. The theoretical tasks could take the form of studies that require the disciple to make a personal application. Below is one example of the studies that I use. Further examples can be found in the Appendix.

Moses the Prophet (Deut. 18:15)

1. It is clearly stated that Moses was a prophet (Hos. 12:12–13). Reflect upon the two functions stated here that Moses performed.
   a) Deliverance
   b) Sustenance
   What do they mean to you?

2. Moses was reluctant to embrace his calling for two reasons.
   a) Exodus 3:11
   b) Exodus 4:10
   What were they? Can you identify with either of them?

Characteristics of Prophetic Ministry (Deut. 18:14–22)

1. The Lord will raise up (v.15). The priesthood continued by physical descent – the prophet by God's

call. Do you see any implications in this for us today?

2. Note the imperative 'I command him' (v.18). The prophetic office seemed to come into being because Israel was afraid of the direct voice of God (v.16). How do you equate in the New Testament all believers hearing God for themselves and prophetic ministry?

3. This warning note is sounded to prevent presumption and to preserve purity of inspiration (v.20). What does presumption mean in this context? How can you avoid it?

When the disciple has completed the study then the discipler should go through it with them. Any errors or mistakes in the understanding should be corrected and the personal element in the answers should be pursued. Practical tasks can be given, such as involving the disciple in praying for others and seeing if they receive a word for them or waiting on God for a word in a specific meeting where you are in attendance. You may also wish to point out to them some object eg a tree, the beach, the hills, a picture etc. Then get them to pray asking God to speak something specific to them using the object as the means through which he communicates. In this way, they can hear God speaking to them using the object as the springboard for a prophetic word. This would be similar to Jeremiah's experience of the potter's house, except that, in his case, God specifically instructed him to go and observe (Jer. 18:1,6).

Once when I was teaching a group of trainees for ministry on the gift of prophecy, I placed on a table an assortment of objects including a book. I divided the group into pairs and, after ensuring that biblical and safe guidelines were in place, I invited them to look at the table of objects. When they felt drawn to a particular item, they were to then ask God what he wanted to say to them through that object, in order to pass it on to their partner. One young man did not have a partner so I invited him to accompany me. After a while, I asked him if he had anything to give me from the Lord. He was rather nervous and said the only thing he was drawn to was the book and felt the Lord said to tell me 'Write the book'. This book you are reading is the result of that prophetic word.

The story that lies behind that incident was as follows. I had been ministering in Christian Fellowship of Columbia, USA, for three months teaching on the prophetic. During this time I met some hurting prophetic people and thought I should write a book on the subject. The title of this book came instantly to mind, 'Healing Earthbound Eagles'. However upon my return to England I lost enthusiasm and impetus for writing the book and did not do anything about it. Then I found myself teaching on the gift of prophecy at the meeting described above, and the rest, as they say, is history.

Whatever practical tasks you assign the disciple, you must not give them the sense that you are looking over their shoulder all the time. Give them room to make mistakes, if need be. In this way, they will probably learn more than if they made no mistakes at all. Theodore Roosevelt once said that the best executives are the ones who have sense enough to pick good men to do what they want done, and enough self restraint to keep from meddling while they do it. Of course, we have to correct afterwards. A good question to keep asking yourself as you disciple someone is this: 'what kind of experiences do others need in order to develop their prophetic calling and gift?' The answer then points the way to the kind of tasks you will set them.

There is great joy in observing the progress and development made in the spiritual life and gifting of those that we have taken the time to disciple.

NOTES

[1]*The Elijah Task,* John & Paula Sandford (Victory House).

[2]*Prophetic Bulletin,* Graham Perrins (Springwood Trust). Used with permission.

Chapter 10

ENTANGLED EAGLES

It may appear strange to leave the problem of sin to the last chapter of this book. Habitual sin or sin that has not been dealt with, in the life of the prophetic person will render them earthbound. So why has this not been mentioned in the chapter on 'Why Eagles Become Earthbound'? My reason, rightly or wrongly, is this: there are other things besides sin, which cause prophetic people to become earthbound, and I wanted to call attention to them first.

It is very easy to attribute all adversity and difficulty in a person's life to sin, when there are other causes responsible. If those other causes are faced and acknowledged, and still the individual is earthbound, then the possibility of sin being the reason cannot be ignored. By taking this approach, I am not implying that one should always leave dealing with sin as the last resort, but I do want to leave the reader with the focus upon Jesus. When we face the issue of sin, it should take us to Jesus as the remedy for it. He is the one that frees us from sin's penalty, sin's power, and finally, sin's presence. As John the Baptist cried: 'Look, the Lamb of God, who takes away the sin of the world!' (John 1:29) or, as the apostle Paul says: 'But where sin increased, grace increased all the more' (Rom 5:20). So, we end this book with an emphasis upon Jesus and the grace of God, through dealing with the problem of sin.

Principally, we are going to deal with those sins, or that sin, over which we seem to have no control and which we keep falling prey to. I once saw a bird that had become entangled by its feet in some netting that was being used to protect growing strawberries. The more the poor bird tried to get free, the more entangled it had become: it was completely unable to fly. The writer of the book of Hebrews exhorts us not to become entangled with sin: 'let us throw off everything that hinders and the sin that so easily entangles, and let us run with perseverance the race marked out for us. Let us fix our eyes on Jesus' (Heb. 12:1–2). Any believers, not just prophetic people, who become entangled with sin, will eventually find themselves unable to move in their gifting. To become entangled in sin means that although we have had our sin cancelled by the cross of Christ, nevertheless, we are still held in the grip and power of it.

We need to experience, in the words of John Wesley's famous hymn, that 'He breaks the power of cancelled sin and sets the prisoner free.' How can this happen? How can we throw off the sin that so easily entangles us? The answer that the writer of the book of Hebrews gives us is to 'fix our eyes on Jesus.' Victory over the power of sin's entanglement comes by looking to Jesus. Before we consider what that means, it will be helpful to remind ourselves how victory over sin is *not* achieved.

Victory over sin is not achieved by having strong willpower alone. This will be good news for those who are aware of the weakness of their willpower.

Determination not to give into temptation, again, will not guarantee that we will not yield to temptation. Many people have become discouraged because, having determined not to give in to temptation, they have fallen into it repeatedly. Neither is victory over sin achieved by threats or prohibitions alone. The whole of the Law of Moses contained threats regarding the consequences of sin, but it never gave anyone the power to stop sinning. It also contained prohibitions. Consider the multitude of commands beginning, 'Thou shalt not', and yet people still were held in the power of sin. The law was good, but it could not give the power necessary to live up to it. If either strong willpower or threats and prohibitions alone could give us victory over sin, then that would demean the cross of Christ.

Victory over sin is achieved by fixing our eyes upon Jesus. That is all very well, I hear you saying, but what does it mean in practice? How do I fix my eyes on Jesus? As mentioned earlier, in Acts 3:1–10, the account is given of Peter and John healing a crippled beggar. Peter and John were on their way to the temple at the time of prayer. At the temple gate called Beautiful sat a crippled beggar. When he saw the two disciples, he asked them for some money. In reply, Peter said: '"Look at us!" So the man gave them his attention, expecting to get something from them' (Acts 3:4–5). To fix our eyes upon Jesus means that we give him our attention, expecting to receive from him the power required to throw off the sin that so easily entangles us. This is to be the continuous pattern of our lives, and not something we do only at the crisis moment of temptation. We must live our lives paying attention to him; being obedient to his word; aligning our lives to his will; listening to his voice and in faith expecting that he will respond with all the help we need to resist sin. Our eyes must come off temptation and onto Jesus. In so doing, a spiritual dynamic is released that will enable us to be free of the power of cancelled sin.

According to Hebrews 11:24–26, Moses refused to be called the son of Pharaoh's daughter and chose to be mistreated along with God's people, suffering disgrace instead of choosing to enjoy the pleasure of sin for a season and having the untold wealth of Egypt. Many commentators and historians believe that Moses was next in line to inherit the throne of Egypt. That would have meant, for him, massive wealth, influence, and power as head of the greatest civilisation on earth at that time. How could he possibly say no to that? The answer given in verse 26 is, 'Because he was looking ahead to his reward'. Moses' eyes were upon something else, and that gave him the strength to say no to the temptation of self-indulgence and self-gratification. Of course, sin has its pleasure in the short term, otherwise no one would ever entertain it. When we are tempted, sin never comes in the guise of something abhorrent or repulsive, but of something to be desired. The sting is this: sin only has pleasure for a season. After that, comes the reckoning, the heartache, the conviction and condemnation, the guilt and the broken relationship with the Lord. As Dr Sam Storms, from Metro Christian Fellowship, Kansas City, USA, said as he preached at a *Passion for Jesus* conference in 1997: 'Sin never looks ugly until you see it in the light of the beauty of Jesus'.

When the temptation to commit sin comes powerfully upon us, with its lying promise of long-term pleasure and gain, it is at that moment that we must believe that a superior joy and pleasure can be had by saying 'no' to temptation and 'yes' to unbroken fellowship with Jesus. Psalm 16:11 says, 'You have made known to me the path of life; you will fill me with joy in your presence, with eternal pleasures at your right hand'. This is not a promise to be enjoyed only in eternity, but a promise of joy and pleasure to be enjoyed now. This is what we must have our eyes upon.

The treadmill of habitual sin will cause us to be earthbound at some point. As prophetic people, we are called to be God's eagles: those that can rise up on the thermals of the Holy Spirit to see his perspective and purpose. Therefore, we must get rid of the entanglements of sin. There are many things that lead to the final entanglement of sin and, as prophetic people, we must be vigilant, so that we do not allow any of these things to gain a foothold in our lives. I have found that prophetic people can be prone to becoming entangled through envy/jealousy.

There is salutary warning against this, in 1 Kings 13:11–32. Here, is the story of an old prophet who lived in Bethel. One day, another prophet, under the direction of the Lord, came to Bethel and prophesied, in King Jeroboam's presence, against the altar that Jeroboam had built. He prophesied of a coming king called Josiah, from the house of David, who would sacrifice the priests of the high places upon it. As a sign that this would all come to pass, he said that the altar would split and the ashes of it spill out. The next moment, the altar split, just as he had said. Jeroboam pointed at the man and cried 'seize him' and as a result, Jeroboam's hand shrivelled up. King Jeroboam asked the prophet to pray for him and, as the prophet prayed, his hand was healed. The sons of the old prophet went and told him all that had happened and at once, the old prophet went after the man of God. Now the Lord had told the man of God that he was not to eat or drink in that place nor return by the way he had come. The old prophet then lied and said that he had had a word from an angel to say that it was alright for the man of God to eat and drink with him in his house. For the man of God's disobedience, judgement was pronounced upon him by the old prophet who, as they were eating together brought a genuine word from the Lord. As the man of God was on his journey home, he was slain by a lion.

On the surface, this seems a strange story until one looks further. It would seem that the old prophet was moved to envy, in that he was resident in Bethel, but when God wanted to speak prophetically in that place he chose someone else from outside to be his mouthpiece. That envy led the old prophet to fabricate a word from the Lord that resulted in the death of the other prophet. Sin had entangled him. It had probably entangled him some time before the event recorded here. Consider the fact that he had been resident in Bethel for some time, and yet had not spoken out about the idolatry of Jeroboam and the false altar. Was this due to fear, or compromise? Whatever the reason, he had accommodated the situation. Then there was the way he deliberately deceived the man of God. It is unlikely that this was the first time he had ever practised deceit. It was possible that this was the result of a bad habit that had been formed in his life over some length of time. He had allowed himself to become truly entangled by sin and had lost the ability to exercise his ministry. This entanglement, together with the envy, led to a lack of integrity which, in turn, led to the death of the younger man.

Prophetic people cannot afford to let envy/jealousy remain in their hearts. Often, it begins through a sense of being passed over or even rejected, in favour of someone else. Then, as the feeling grows, so does the desire to discredit others or speak untruth about them. Although this will probably not lead to anyone's death, it will certainly cause an inability to flow in the prophetic gift. Like all Christians, prophetic people must be ruthless in their dealing with sin.

Another sin that will keep a prophetic person earthbound, if not dealt with, is bitterness. Bitterness is not a one-off sinful act, it is a sinful state or attitude ongoing in a person's life. According to Ephesians 4:30–31, bitterness grieves the Holy Spirit, so how can we expect that he will continue to grant us uninterrupted revelation, unless we cease to grieve him. When we become aware that our inability to flow in the prophetic is caused by being entangled with sin, we must first confess it to God: no denying it or hiding it; no making excuses for it. We must honestly admit that we have sinned and are guilty before him. We must own up. Then we need to repent before God of that which has entangled us for so long. To repent is not the same as to regret it. We do not repent because we regret the fact that we are earthbound as a result of sin. To truly repent means, we change our mind: we come to a new way of thinking about sin, especially that which entangles us. We turn from our way of thinking to God's way and thoroughly agree with him. Having done this, we need to ask for his cleansing and forgiveness, which he assures us we will receive. For 'if we confess our sins, he is faithful and just and will forgive us our sins and purify us from all unrighteousness' (1 John 1:9).

There is also another reason for becoming earthbound that is an integral part of being entangled by sin and that is, shame. The shame we experience inwardly as we know how much our sin grieves the Holy Spirit; the shame we feel in case anyone finds out what we are really like or are up to; the shame that is linked to our sense of failure in not overcoming sin; and the shame in our failure to fulfil our calling. The writer to the Hebrews says that Jesus scorned the shame of the cross

(Heb.12:2). The cross in Jesus' day was a vile repugnant symbol of shame. Most literature of the time omitted any reference to the cross because it was so vile. It was designed, not merely to kill, but also to crush a person physically, mentally and emotionally. It brought scandal to the family of the one crucified. Most victims were crucified naked, and no Roman citizen could be crucified because of the shame associated with it. Jesus scorned all of this shame in order that you might not have to carry shame in your life. He died for our sins and he died for the shame that they cause. It is for this reason that he is the lifter of our heads (Ps. 3:3). There is a familiar saying in English, that 'we hang our heads in shame', but Jesus bestows glory upon us and lifts up our head. He reverses, completely, the effects of shame and removes shame itself from me. Hallelujah! This is the good news of the gospel that we embrace, and yet, too many Christians feel that their sins and failures are too great, or have been committed too often, for them to be able to receive forgiveness. If we think or feel like this then, in essence, we are saying that our sins and our shame are too great for the death of Jesus to pay for them. This is really a sin of pride, although most would not recognise it as being so. In reality, what such a person is saying is, 'the cross of Christ was not sufficient nor good enough to pay or deal with *my* sins'. In effect, such a person is exalting themselves (sins, shame and failure) above the cross. This kind of thinking or, perhaps more accurately, this kind of feeling, for the problem lies in our emotions rather than in our intellect, needs to be repented of and changed, otherwise the person will find themselves constantly entangled.

There is another side to this for some Christians. They *feel* they need to do penance. They feel that their sin, shame, and failure was so bad, when they ought to have known better, that although they have genuinely repented, they must now either feel very bad for a few days or else engage in some form of righteous deeds in order to prove themselves. They grovel or work harder for acceptance by God, instead of accepting the wonderful, unconditional forgiveness offered through Jesus to those who repent. We are exhorted in Hebrews to throw off the entanglement of sin by fixing our eyes upon Jesus. We are also exhorted to fix our eyes upon him in order to rid ourselves of shame. Any focal point or fixation other than Jesus, will keep us entangled in sin and shame, but 'those who look to him are radiant; their faces are never covered with shame' (Ps. 34:5).

Perhaps, outside of the Scriptures, no other words express this truth so clearly as those of an old chorus:

Turn your eyes upon Jesus,
Look full in his wonderful face,
And the things of earth,
Will grow strangely dim,
In the light of his glory and grace.

Prophetic people, God's eagles, will have little to fear in regard to their gifting and their ability to soar again, if they adjust the focus of their living so that in all things it is Jesus that has the pre-eminence. Keeping Jesus pre-eminent in our ministry and ministering will help to ensure that the fire of the Holy Spirit does not go out. For the Spirit will always bring glory to Jesus: that is part of his ministry.

Paul, when writing to the Thessalonians, in 1 Thessalonians 5:19–20, tells them of a way in which they can put out the Spirit's fire. 'Do not put out the Spirit's fire; do not treat prophecies with contempt'. The word 'contempt', as used here, means to regard as nothing; to treat as of no account. When the church or the individual disregards prophetic utterances over a period of time, then the fire of the Spirit will eventually go out. Surely no Christian or local church wilfully desires such a thing to happen, and yet sadly, at times, the fire does go out: God's eagles become earthbound or are kept earthbound. Instead, let us resolve, by his grace, to keep the Spirit's fire burning. Let us not, through fear, insecurity, or even familiarity, do anything to hinder the prophetic gift from operating in our midst. Rather, let us encourage, advise, and stir up, the use of the gift of prophecy and prophetic ministry in our churches.

Eagles – soar again. Do not be afraid of loving correction: it will enable you to soar even higher. You are needed in the church, especially in the days in which we are living. The Holy Spirit is being poured out throughout the Earth in an unprecedented way, and that means redeemed people will prophesy. That means you will prophesy. It is time to fly again. You can and you will, and may this result in Ephesians 3:21 being true in your church: 'to him be glory in the church and in Christ Jesus throughout all generations, for ever and ever! Amen'.

APPENDIX

Examples Of Studies Used In Discipling People In The Prophetic

Study 1. Essential Foundations

The following words relating to Prophecy were in use in secular Greek:

Prophetes   Prophetis   Propheteuo   Propheteia
Prophetikos   Pseudo Prophetes   Mantis

1. With the aid of *Kittel's Theological Dictionary of New Testament Words* or a good lexicon, look up those words and draw conclusions as to the understanding of prophecy people would have had at that time.

2. How does the Scripture qualify the meaning of any of the above terms?

3. How does the context affect the word 'prophet' in the following?
   Titus 1:12   Luke 22:64   John 4:19

4. When the New Testament speaks of a false prophet, does it normally refer to
   a) a false claim?
   b) false content?
   Refer to Mark 13:22 and 1 John 4:1 and give your reasons.

Study 2. What is a Prophet in the Old Testament?

1. What was the earliest term for Prophet (1 Sam. 9:9)? What did this mean?

2. The usual term for Prophet in the Old Testament was 'Nabi'. In Arabic it means: to proclaim. In Hebrew it means: to bubble forth (see Prov. 18:4). In Accadian it means: to call or be called. In the LXX the Greek word (Prophetes) means: to speak before. Putting the earliest term (in 1 Sam. 9:9) together with 'Nabi', describe the dual aspect of the Prophet.

3. Nabi is first used in Genesis 20:7.
   a) What activity is linked to the prophet here?
   b) What functional aspect of the prophet precedes prayer (see Gen. 18:17,23. c/f Amos 3:7)?
   c) What is your own experience, if any, of this and how can you apply this to your experience?

4. In the following Scriptures, the prophets do not adopt a fatalistic approach to prayer, but rather, one of dialogue: Exodus 32:7–14; Numbers 14:10–19; 1 Samuel 12:19–23.
   a) What is your experience of dialogue prayer?
   b) What insights can you glean from the above Scriptures?

Study 3. Jeremiah's Prophetic Calling

1. Jeremiah was reluctant to accept the prophetic call (Jer. 1:5–6).
   a) What were his reasons for this?
   b) What causes you to have reluctance in embracing your prophetic calling?

2. It is clear, from verse 5, that prophetic ministry is an undoubted calling from God. More than anything else, a prophet's training is through his life experiences, not just formal instruction.
   a) Which biblical prophets illustrate this?
   b) Choose one and do a study of their life?
   c) How do you see the context of your past life as equipping you for prophetic ministry?

3. In Jeremiah 1:7, God speaks of specific, divine direction. Prophets must know that they have the freedom to respond. Prophetic ministry is stifled when prophets are over-controlled by others.
   a) How can prophets today be free to respond, yet remain submitted and accountable to leadership?
   b) Suggest practical ways to accomplish this.

Study 4. Jeremiah and the Words of God

1. The prophetic has both a negative and positive side
   (Jer.1:10).
   a) In this verse, why is the negative spoken?
   b) What should follow a negative word?

2. When Jeremiah said, 'I do not know how to speak'
   (v.6), he expressed understanding that proclamation is
   the vital expression of prophetic ministry.
   a) What are we to proclaim (v.7,9)?
   b) The prophet is God's spokesman, but what does it
   mean to speak the words of God?

BIBLIOGRAPHY

Bickle, Mike. *Growing in the Prophetic* (Kingsway, 1995)

Bromily, Geoffrey W. *Theological Dictionary of the New Testament* (Eerdmans/Paternoster)

Clarke, Adam. *The Master Christian Library: Daniel* CD-ROM (Sage Software)

Cooke, Graham. *Developing Your Prophetic Gifting* (Sovereign World, 1994)

Cornwall, Judson. *Leaders, Eat What You Serve* (Destiny Image)

Damazio, Frank. *Developing the Prophetic Ministry* (Bible Temple, 1983)

Fee, Gordon D. *God's Empowering Presence* (Hendrickson, 1994)

Garret, Clive. *Proclaim* (Springwood Trust)

Grudem, Wayne. *The Gift of Prophecy in the New Testament Today* (Kingsway, 1988)

The Hodder Bible Handbook (Hodder & Stoughton)

Houston, Graham. *Prophecy Now* (Inter Varsity Press, 1989)

Jamieson, Faussett & Brown. *The Bethany Parallel Commentary on the New Testament* (Bethany House, 1983)

Kreider, Alan. *Journey Towards Holiness* (Marshall Pickering, 1986)

Perrins, Graham. *Prophetic Bulletin* (Springwood Trust, 1992)

Randolph, Larry J. *User-Friendly Prophecy* (Destiny Image, 1998)

Rea, John. *The Holy Spirit in the Bible* (Marshall Pickering, 1992)

165

Sandford, John and Paula. *The Elijah Task* (Victory House, 1977)

Snyder, James L. *In Pursuit of God: The Life of A.W. Tozer* (Christian Publications, 1991)

Strong, James. *Strong's Exhaustive Concordance* (Thomas Nelson, 1990)

The Westminster Dictionary of the Bible (Westminster Press/Collins)

Wood, Leon J. *The Prophets of Israel* (Baker Book House, 1979)